The Book on Account-Based Marketing

Practical Tips for Exponential Revenue Growth

Bassem Hamdy

The Book on Account-Based Marketing: Practical
Tips for Exponential Revenue Growth

ISBN: 9781980474906

Cover creation by Creativelog.

Table of Contents

Table of Contents

To my wife, Katie, who has heard every twist, turn, and all the intrigue in the world of B2B marketing — and at least pretended to be interested.

The Foundations of Account-Based Marketing

"Wanting something is not enough. You must hunger for it. Your motivation must be absolutely compelling in order to overcome the obstacles that will invariably come your way."
– Les Brown

The most important thing for you to realize from the outset is that this is not a book about marketing. The world of business-to-business revenue generation has evolved to the point that, no matter what your functional role, account-based marketing (ABM) will play a pivotal part in your individual and company's success or failure.

Are you in sales? Account-based marketing will be the single largest component of the quality of revenue that you generate. Are you in customer success? Account-based marketing will be the foundation of your overall customer satisfaction. Are you in marketing? Account-based marketing will be the most highly leveraged tool in your arsenal of tools.

My First Attempt at Account-Based Marketing

I know this because, through the course of my nineteen-year history in marketing – in both startups and Fortune 500 companies – account-based marketing has been the determinant of my professional success. Twenty years ago, I began my career in the financial services industry. I threw my hat in the air at my college graduation, and within twenty-four hours, I was on a flight to London to join the emerging markets desk of a prominent bank in the United Kingdom. At the time, I believed this to be the start of a life-long career in finance. However, it took me less than a month to realize this was a major mistake. After that, it took me nearly a year to be honest with myself about the situation and take the leap to something else.

Knowing that banking was not for me, I dove towards the opposite extreme. I traveled back to North America and joined the furthest thing from an established bank: a bootstrapped startup. I traded in my suit and advisory role, and in exchange donned a t-shirt, jeans, and sandals for a hands-on implementation role. Since I was wrong about my previous long-term career, I approached this startup as a temporary assignment. My goal was to get the lay of the land, lick my wounds, and figure out my next step. I told my friends that I would be there for just a few months, but I ended up staying there for over fifteen years. While I started in a position in which I was implementing a single product, I eventually became the Chief Marketing Officer, responsible for all matters of pre-sales, cloud sales, product development, marketing, and advertising.

My journey with this company was one of the greatest adventures of my life, and it was an opportunity for which I will always be eternally grateful. In addition to meeting friends and colleagues who would play a vital role in the future of my career, it gave me insights into every aspect of a business-to-business company. This unique vantage point served me throughout my career.

I eventually moved from this bootstrapped startup to a venture-capital-backed startup. I learned that the only difference between these two extremes of the financing spectrum is velocity. At the VC-backed startup, I found myself employing the same tactics that had previously made me successful. However, with the benefit of financial backing, I was able to achieve in three-years what it had taken me a decade to achieve previously. The additional cash flow and resources of this second startup provided exceptional momentum to accelerate my actions, but the strategy and tactics involved were identical.

With successful experience in a bootstrapped startup and then in a VC-backed startup, I was privileged to be able to spend the next stint of my time as a professional "dabbler." I met with a variety of companies at various stages in their development, and I consulted with them to help them unlock their next level of success. This work provided an exceptional amount of exposure: exposure to different teams and strategies of working, as well as exposure to every sort of product imaginable. Amidst this background of variability, however, I noticed one striking consistency: the tactics I used in each of these diverse companies were remarkably similar.

I'm grateful for the shifting paradigms my career has afforded me. I've moved from a technology company in Canada to a technology company in California. I've rolled up my sleeves and done every facet of marketing, and at other times I've had over one hundred marketers reporting to me. From this vantage point, I've learned from my experiences that even with minimal funding and a tiny team, you can overcome seemingly insurmountable obstacles and succeed. Ultimately, it has nothing to do with how much money you have to spend. Rather, it has everything to do with being smart about how and where you spend the money you have. The only difference that venture capital makes is the speed at which you achieve your goal. However, a jetpack can get you twice as lost when you are headed in the wrong direction.

Most recently, I've entered into a new adventure: entrepreneurship. Having seen first-hand the experience of bootstrapping a startup as well as raising financing, I decided to try my hand at starting a company. I launched a digital consultancy and am ecstatic to help incredible companies grow their brand, while I also grow my consulting practice.

I've defined my career as a revenue marketer. While revenue marketing has the power to transform a company in any industry, there are three unifying principles that I have observed.

Principle #1: My number is your number

As a marketer, whenever I talk to salespeople, I always start with one simple truth: my number is your number. Whatever your number may be, that is the shared reality that we both hold. There is no "sales" silo or "marketing" silo – we are in this together. That's why, in my career, I have never focused on one number, the revenue goal. Lead generation numbers, AKA lead counts, or a lead velocity make me queasy. I hear about these numbers at every conference I attend, every podcast I listen to, and every book I read; people become hyper-focused on Marketing Qualified Leads (MQLs), even though that is not what real revenue teams look at when they're trying to grow a company. A strong marketer shares the same fundamentals as a strong salesperson. After all, if a marketer can't sell to one person, how can they sell to thousands of people?

Principle #2: I am a promise-keeper

The next principle I always share is that I am a promise-keeper. This is critical to customer success and business integrity. Too often, I see companies that, accidentally or on purpose, are only playing "short game." They become so obsessed with making the next sale that they become promise-makers. Does the customer want a feature we don't have yet? No problem—of course, we have that feature! Does the customer expect extra support you know you can't provide? It's ok—promise them whatever will get them through the door, and worry about it later! These decisions, regardless of how small they seem at the time, are irresistible; for many companies, they are inherently disastrous. These quick and simple promises facilitate the top of the sales funnel, but ultimately leave the customer stranded high and dry, trying to figure out what to do. Of course, this kind of revenue generation is antithetical to high-quality marketing.

I encourage you to commit to being a promise-keeper. Deliver on every single promise you make. As a marketer, adopt the mindset of a customer success rep, and endeavor to never let your client down. While this is difficult to do in the moment, it is a guaranteed way to succeed in the long run. Shattered promises line the road to a company's demise.

Principle #3: The future is longer than one quarter

When you look at the world from a quarterly or monthly number perspective, you end up making some really bad decisions. Back in my days at a bootstrapped startup, there was often—quite literally— a constant focus on the next month. There were many times when we were worried about making payroll and keeping the lights on. In these times, it becomes common sense to focus on the next month, week, or even day.

More often than not, though, companies focus on the short-term even when they are not in this sort of dire situation. It is the equivalent of a company's fight/flight/freeze response. The members of the team imagine they are in a life or death scenario, even though they are on a routine sales call or marketing exercise. While this thinking may keep a company afloat in those rare times of crisis, they are more likely than not to lead to bankruptcy at most others.

Here is a truth that I have found: sometimes you have to forgo short-term revenue for the good of the business. Sometimes, to grow the business successfully, you need to behave responsibly for the company, even if it is to your detriment. Because of this, I always emphasize that you have to force your vision beyond your quarterly bonus and promise the organization that you are going to look at not just this quarter's revenue, but next quarter's, and next year's. You have to have a plan and a strategy that allows that to happen.

How this Relates to Account-Based Marketing

Let's talk about my first attempt at account-based marketing. So, picture this: I'm at a very small software company with a handful of clients. It's just a few years past the dawn of a new millennium, and competition is fierce. Think about it: there was Oracle, SAP, PeopleSoft, and JD Edwards, each of which had thousands of employees and a worldwide reputation. We, on the other hand, were an unknown startup with a dozen ragtag team members. In spite of the odds stacked against us, we were trying to coin a brand-new term: Construction ERP. Launching a new product category was a monumental task, one which required taking what was basic account software and transforming it into a cross-department platform.

We were confident in our product. We had the best product, but nobody knew about us. How could we ever hope to compete with the likes of these monstrous software companies? They were marketing machines. They spent more on advertising in one month than I did in two years! I'm pretty sure they spent more on office supplies than our entire marketing personnel and advertising budget! Everywhere I went, I saw our competitors. Driving to work, I would see a billboard for Oracle. Watching TV, I would see an advertisement for SAP. There were countless nights when I felt helpless; my marketing team consisted of two employees and me, and all three of us carried additional responsibilities beyond just marketing. During this time, my life became a blur of activity; I was constantly on the road doing product demos while still working as a solution engineer and building our product roadmap. Needless to say, time was an exceptionally valuable and rare commodity.

Since I came from a finance background, I viewed myself as a math person. So I said, "Let me break this down and figure out how to sell, market, and be better. What's the most efficient way to get there?" I took a step back and realized how much time I was wasting each day. Then, I realized I wasn't alone: I saw the sales team wasting time as well. They were spending hours each day speaking with people who weren't ideal personas and weren't working at ideal target companies either.

I started to look at our customers from a numbers perspective. While we were a startup specifically in the construction industry, we were also just a startup. As anyone at a startup can attest, startups will sell to anyone. Given how tight money was, the best deal was the deal that gave us cash flow. We even sold to a coconut processing plant in the Caribbean. No company was too small to consider; no lead was too insignificant to talk to. While this did lead to a trickle of income, it came at the expense of a deluge of time. It was as if we were spending every second looking for loose change under every couch cushion while never putting together a strategy to go after the real dollars.

One weekend, I locked myself in a room and thought, *rather than going after everyone, what type of companies do I want to sell to?* Out of the tens of thousands of companies, I analyzed and picked apart every aspect of who these companies were. Finally, I began to see a pattern, and I realized that only a few particular types of companies made sense. At last, the ocean of possibility was whittled down to just about one thousand companies. After playing with my assumptions further, I was able to pare this down to about four hundred specific companies. This process, while exhausting, made me feel like I had shed sixty pounds overnight. Rather than running around trying to talk to every person at every company, I now had a compact "hit list" of the most desirable companies with which to work.

The next thing I did was determine the best point of contact to approach at each of these four hundred companies. After the gigantic undertaking of selecting companies, this step was relatively simple. We were selling a highly complex accounting solution, which required surgeon-like precision to implement. As a result, I knew that we needed to get in front of one of just a handful of executives at each of these companies. What began as "boiling the ocean" was starting to feel more like laser-precision targeting. At this point, I knew that I needed to talk to key executives, and I needed to talk to 400 to 1000 companies. With these details in hand, I started to research each of these companies, digging in to see what each of these companies did.

At the time, I didn't know anything about market research and how to approach this sort of problem. As they say, "necessity is the mother of all skill." While my approach may not have been conventional, I made up for it in effort and enthusiasm! I started simply; every time I went to a construction company; I would look at the magazines that filled their office. It may seem absurd now, but back in 2003, print magazines were still an accurate indication of where people were directing their attention. I would sit down and look through the stack of magazines in their office, and pretty soon I found a consistent trend. Virtually every office I visited had a copy of a magazine called *Engineering News-Record.*

ENR is a weekly publication, considered the *Time* magazine of the construction industry. It contained the best data for the industry and was held in high esteem by most of the industry insiders. More importantly, the price to advertise within *Engineering News Record* was even within the grasp of our tiny, bootstrapped startup. After making a few calls, I realized that we would be able to afford a quarter page ad in this weekly publication for exactly $10,000. At the time, that seemed like an unbelievable sum of money. The thought of spending $10,000—more than I had spent on every marketing initiative combined—on just three inches of paper in an obscure magazine was terrifying.

I called the publisher and said, "We are just a small startup that is trying to change the world and do big things in the construction industry. Is there anything you could do to help us out?" She said that she would be happy to help me out for the tidy sum of $10,000. My heart sunk, and I told her that there was no way we could afford that. But then I had an idea. I realized that $10,000 would get me in front of over 250,000 readers of this magazine. From my homework, however, I knew that I only cared about four hundred to one thousand of those readers. That wasn't too much. So, I got in my car and drove to the publisher to implore my case in person.

Once I arrived, I rushed up the stairs and met with the lady who I had spoken with on the phone. I explained my situation to her as succinctly as I could: your magazine is the most respected journal in the entire industry, and you've got an incredible readership of over

250,000 individuals. However, my company is just trying to get in front of one thousand of those readers. Could we redirect those specific subscribers and stitch in a 4-page glossy insert?

We couldn't rely on someone seeing our advertisement once and reaching out to us. I was hoping three times might do the trick. I asked (begged) her to go through that stitching process three times. Then I begged some more. Then I groveled. She either got exhausted from my begging or felt sorry for me. Either way, eventually she agreed. She called her printer, and he said that it would be simple to support my request. The line went quiet for a few moments, and then they both erupted in laughter. Why on earth would anyone want to advertise to just a tiny fraction of their overall readership? But I had done my homework and was confident in my numbers.

Starting in early January, we pulled the issues for these one thousand people. We hand-stitched in our four-page advertisement and returned them to the magazine for distribution. We repeated this process the next week. And we repeated it the week after that. And then, on the fourth week, we sent a simple postcard to each of these one thousand people with a straightforward explanation of who we were and why we wanted to work with them. And it paid off –seeing our advertisement three weeks in a row caused an overwhelming percentage of these one thousand people to reach out to us. It was a relatively simple tactic, but it crushed our competition.

No one in our industry had taken this novel approach to advertising. We took the same amount of money that would have bought us a quarter page ad in one magazine issue. By using creativity and thinking outside of the box, we stretched this budget into three highly-targeted advertisements. And the result? We went from negligible market share to 20% market share. We grew our revenue by tenfold. And we went from being a footnote in an industry to one of the most dominant players around.

What still surprises me is how simple this action was, yet how extreme the results were. And it all boiled down to my roots in finance. I knew how to leverage $1 to yield the maximum return on investment. Rather than spreading that $1 to advertise to every possible company, it was exponentially more effective to deploy the dollar against an ad that would target the specific person to whom I most wanted to speak. Although the exact implementation of this core premise changed over time, this key insight never varied. And while it solved the problem of how to remain in business, it opened up all sorts of new problems, like how to keep track of these one thousand companies. That was a more interesting problem to me. Again, as a bootstrapped startup worker, I started to address it in the simplest way possible: with a spreadsheet.

Picture a spreadsheet with one thousand rows, each filled with information from a different company. I knew that the company information was not enough. We were selling accounts, but at the end of the day, accounts don't buy; people buy.

But what people should we be targeting? That's where the persona stage came in – this is the first time I had to understand the standard organizational chart for a target company. I started by looking at all the emails and phone calls that we sent to clients. In review, I found out the quickest path to the deal was to talk to a financial leader, then an operations leader, and finally talk to IT.

My spreadsheet (our first real ABM tool) was almost complete. I had the X-axis—the companies that we wanted to engage with—and on the Y-Axis, I had all the ideal roles with whom we needed to talk.

- X-Axis: The company information – Name, Location, Markets Served
- Y-Axis: Ideal point of contact title at each company (Vice President of Finance/CFO, Vice President of Operations, Vice President of Human Resources)

The Formula

Now we knew which companies we needed to talk to and the people at the company we needed to talk to, but that wasn't enough.

What we needed was an account-based score that would tell the company—the entire company, not just the sales and marketing departments—the trust status of every account. I created a simple points system, through which each account could get a total of ten points. Half of the points were based on engagement, and the other half on the opportunity. I then created a very basic math equation: If there was no activity, then the account had zero points. If we spoke to people at the account in the last 90 days, but not the "right" people, the account gained one point. And finally, if we started to speak to the right people, the account got one point per major target contacts. When an account hit 4+ points, it went from Red to Yellow on the big board; above seven points, it went from yellow to green.

What was amazing was that the entire company could see this scorecard. Everyone from the individual contributor to the chairman checked the spreadsheet and would rally around all the greens, making the deal happen. Focus matters. When the company became a won opportunity, it turned to purple.

Even though we were still just a tiny startup, I'll never forget those first meetings I held. I would go into a company's office, and they would say, "Hey, oh my God, you guys are everywhere! You're so much better than these other companies; you must be doing so well! You must be driving Oracle crazy!" I would smile and nod, all the while knowing that we were just a handful of people working out of a tiny office.

As time went on, I tried different tactics. I hosted major events to attract my key prospects and closed deals before the event ended. I hosted elaborate dinner parties reminiscent of a Great Gatsby-era gala. Instead of hosting these events to see Daisy, they were meant to lure in my ideal customers. We knew our ideal customer well enough to know the type of events that they couldn't refuse, and we used these events to forge lasting relationships. We even researched to find the route that a

Chief Executive Officer would take on their drive home from work, and we bought billboard advertisements for them to see on their drives home. The goal of each of these different tactics was to make our target customer think, "Hey, these guys must be the real deal."

We took all the oxygen out of the room. We were inventing the playbook as we went, and not everything worked. But some things did. And the things that did are now the stories we tell at bars and when we reminisce about "the good old days." That is one of the aspects that I most appreciate about account-based marketing: it puts the fun into business-to-business marketing.

I realize that account-based marketing is a strange nomenclature. At the end of the day, it is a result rather than a process. It's not about marketing, but rather about having singular goals that align your entire organization. It is about creating an experience—account-based experiences—and it is the fastest and most efficient way I know of to generate more revenue.

The Thin Line that Separates Success From Failure

The most important thing to realize is that the question of success or failure hinges around whether or not your revenue team is aligned. In many ways, "revenue team" is a new term in the world of marketing. While the phrase may be new, the underlying concept is ancient. Quite simply, the concept of a revenue team involves three foundational elements of a company: the sales team, the marketing team, and the customer success team. Rather than framing each of these as distinct parts of an organization, the idea of a "revenue team" is shifting the paradigm towards the perspective that that these three groups are inextricably linked. To treat these groups as separate and distinct is to approach a marathon as a three-legged race. You may get to the finish line, but it will be far more awkward and complicated than necessary. On the other hand, if you embrace the concept that these three groups succeed or fail together, you take a step towards turning a marathon into a relay race. You realize that each piece holds the key to the other's success. Rather than disparate parts with competing goals, these groups are part of an intricately orchestrated event.

This concept is so dear to me that for every organization I lead, I hold daily "revenue team standup meetings." In these daily meetings, I gather the key leaders of the sales team, the marketing team, and the customer success team. We take turns going around the room, and each member shares what they accomplished yesterday, what they plan to accomplish today, and any task that may impede their progress today, all as briefly as possible. This allows every leader to understand the entire organization's priorities, and it ensures that no one is accidentally blocking the progress of another revenue team member. It increases appreciation of the other components of our team and keeps us all pushing in the same direction.

If your company is not yet doing a revenue team standup, how often are you talking? Are you relying on Salesforce.com to lead towards this alignment? If so, I've got bad news for you: that's never going to happen. Alignment means trust. That is, trust in each other to make mistakes and run your plays. Alignment means space to experiment. It means giving the sales team room to experiment and make mistakes. Letting the marketing team take risks and learn from their failures. Providing support for the customer support team to try new things and learn from unexpected setbacks.

A revenue team doesn't just have *shared* goals; it has *aligned* goals. The revenue number is the goal. There's a mathematical formula on how you get to the number. And getting there means that you have to have that same goal. That fact applies as much to customer acquisition as it does to customer retention. Software as a Service (SAAS) companies should be tracking metrics like renewal rates and churn rates.

Alignment between sales, marketing, and customer success is the covenant that delineates the separation between success and failure for a revenue team. When I look back on my eighteen-year history, I have heard multiple anecdotal stories about a lack of alignment. The lack of alignment comes from simply not understanding each other. Since this is so important, I have compiled three letters to each of the leaders for the sales, marketing, and customer success team. Feel free to read the letter that applies to your respective role, and to skip the others. However, if you have the time and have the ambition to lead a revenue team, I recommend that you read the other chapters as well. Not only will this give you empathy for the other components of the revenue team, but it will also help you better understand how you can support each of them. After all, your team will survive and thrive together, or die together.

Letter to Sales Leadership

Dear Sales Executive,
You are great. Nobody's trying to take away how you can close that deal. But I will tell you a secret: marketing isn't easy either. Neither is supporting clients. Nor is it easy to create all the collateral that you present in sales pitches, or to draft the emails that help you follow-up with prospects. Each of these groups—marketing, customer success, and sales support—is doing their best to help you score that critical goal. More importantly, they are looking past the immediate goal and thinking about how to build a world-class company. The more that you understand the marketer's heart and mind, the more you will be able to exceed your quota and maximize your commission. Marketing, customer success, and sales support each want to build a lasting and respectable brand.

Take a marketer on a sales call and get them to see what potential customers are saying. Help them understand the work that you do in order to educate a sales prospect. Let

Let them hear the objections that you face, and see the level of ambiguity that you confront on a daily basis. As you go through these challenges together, remember that you are a team and that you are sharing the same goal. There will be many trying days. There will be sales calls where the marketer pushes back on the deal that you're trying to close. When that pushback comes, rather than being annoyed or ignoring them, realize that there may be a strong reason. The marketer has gone through account-based training, and they know the type of client your company needs for long-term success. Chance are, the deal they object to is not aligned with your company's goal. While they may cost you a few deals in the short-term, their objections are leading to your company's long-term success. You may very well thank them down the road for saving you heartache and keeping your company prospering.

Few people in life face as much rejection, doubt, and skepticism as you do on a daily basis. As a salesperson, you are a different breed. You are called to remain optimistic and always set your sites on the next objective. You are critical to your company's success, and you are the tip of the spear, expanding your company's empire. But know that you cannot achieve victory alone. While you close deals and drive revenue growth, you need your team to keep your customers happy. Without that, you wouldn't have a strong reputation on which to continue to grow your brand. And you also need your team to spread the word about your victories. This leads to more wind in your sail, and it will help you get to your destination faster. Building a company is a team sport, and the more that you can collaborate with your teammates, the stronger you will be.

Letter to Marketing Leadership

Dear Marketer Exccutivc,
I know that deep down in your bones, it doubtlessly feels that you are smarter than every single salesperson in your company. It is so tempting to believe this. Please, resist the temptation to think this. It's true that you are a creative genius. You take incomprehensibly complex topics and distill them into easily digestible narratives. It's true that you are a strategic mastermind. You take in the big picture and set a comprehensive direction that enables long-term success. However, your company wouldn't be in existence were it not for the increased revenue and customer reference points that your sales team makes possible.

As a marketer, you maintain a fine balance between today's number and tomorrow's number. You know that to focusing on today's metric at the expense of tomorrow's will lead to failure. And you also know that focusing on tomorrow's number without achieving your key metrics today may mean that you never get to see tomorrow. You have the onerous position of setting your team's cadence and equalizing the demand to meet today's goal with the duty to sustain your team for tomorrow's battle as well. To help maintain this balance, go on a sales call with a salesperson and see what they go through on a daily basis. Hear first-hand the objections they face.

objections they face. Recognize what messages connect with sales prospects and which ones land flat. Get a sense for your company's sales cycle and for how long it takes to acquire a new customer. Celebrate the positive reactions from a sales prospect, and feel good about the incredible brand that you're helping to build. While the salesperson may seem like the adversary, take comfort in knowing that you share a common enemy: the competition. Realize that you're on the same team and that the salesperson does not have an easy job. Maybe even hug a salesperson—they may need it.

After that, spend some time with your customer success team. See the work that they do to keep your customers happy. Witness that when customers have a bad day, calling the customer support person may be the easiest way for them to blow off some steam. Pay attention to how easy it is to complain to a customer success person, but how rarely they hear from customers when things are going well. Hug the customer success worker too—they may need it. After all, without their constant attention to your customers, you wouldn't have the case studies, success stories, positive reputation, and referrals that keep your brand alive.

Letter to Customer Success Leadership

Dear Customer Success Manager,
You may have the hardest job of all. When things are going perfectly, you're likely to hear the least from your customers. If you perform your job flawlessly, there is rarely a ticker-tape parade. However, if you make one

mistake, your customers are sure to let you know, and loudly at that. Even worse, even when things aren't your fault, you're likely to be blamed. It can be easy to feel like the world is out to get you. And to make matters worse, it can often feel like the salespeople and marketing people on your team are out to get you too. As much as you can, realize that the sales team and marketing team are on your side.

Even though it may seem like it, the sales team is not trying to overpromise to a client just to add more work to your to-do list. Just as you have metrics you need to meet, they do too. Be as supportive as you can and understand that sometimes, in the heat of battle on the sales floor or in an office conference room, things happen. Promises are made, agreements are struck, and salespeople do what they need to in order to keep the lights on. That doesn't mean you need to let salespeople off the hook for overpromising, but do try your best to work with them to make sure that the revenue sticks.

I know it can be easy to remain quiet in revenue team meetings. The salespeople can beat their chests and hoot and holler. It can be easy to let them talk over you. But at the end of the day, they need to hear what your customers are saying. They need to know the types of customers who love you and the types of customers who are more trouble than they are worth. You hold the keys to each salesperson's success and to your company's success. It's up to you to help them understand who your ideal customer is and how you can find more of them. This skill will make the difference between success and failure for your company.

Your marketing team needs this information as well. They need to understand what makes your product and service so successful. They also need to know what other pain-points your customers are experiencing. That insight may lead to your company's next killer feature or amazing new product. They need to understand how your customers think what conferences are they attending, what trade publications are they reading, where are they finding out about new companies? This is vital information that will help marketers find more customers like your favorite customer.

Bringing it all Together

I hope that you're realizing that the process is a three-act play. And hopefully, at the end of it, you'll have the tools to make account-based marketing work. Nothing is a dream. There is no magic bullet here. But the beauty of ABM is its truth. It is focused. It builds consensus. It rewards the highest-value work product from a team working in concert. But the most important thing about ABM is that it's about honesty. And that honesty starts with you, and every team member, being brutally honest with yourself and your company. You have to turn off the echo chamber. It is easy to be lulled into a false sense of security: we are the best company in our space. Why? Well...because we're the best. We are better than the competitors. Why? Because...we're awesome! You need to dismiss all the feel-good platitudes and be completely and objectively honest about your company's strengths and weaknesses. Only once you set this aside can you be honest about where you are and in what direction you need to head.

The account-based marketing journey is a three-act process. Act I is about self-knowledge. Act II is about strategy and execution. Act III is about exploding your revenue. Act I is without a doubt the hardest. It requires that you stop seeing everything you learned in college or business school as the answer. It's about radical conversations. It's about being honest about yourself, but it also gives you a chance to psych yourself up. Being truthful can give you an understanding of what your goals need to be.

Sometimes when I talk to companies, they say, "You know what? We want to start selling the big whales. We want to start selling the big guys, and we're going to focus on account-based marketing to make that happen."

I always start by asking them the same basic question: "Does your product hold up against the largest competitors in your industry?" Invariably they answer, "No, not really." I then ask them: "Do you offer the same level of service?" Nearly every time the answer is the same: "No, not at all." About this time, I can see that the wheels are starting to turn. I ask them one final question:

"Alright, so what makes you think account-based marketing is going to work?"

Hopefully, they don't say, "Well, I read your book." What they say is, "We don't know. We hope focus matters." And if so, I tell them, "Focus does matter, and that's what's going to happen. But first of all, turn the spotlight on yourself. Stop fooling yourself in an attempt to feel good. Start to be honest about what's working, and more importantly, be honest about what is preventing you from being the dominant player in your market. Find out what your company is really made of." This brings them to the very first step, which is to determine to whom you are really selling. We'll examine this in our next section.

Key Takeaways:
- Regardless of whether you are a single-person bootstrapped startup or a hundred-person venture-backed company, the tactics you use will be the same. Account-based marketing is the most efficient way to identify and obtain your target customer.
- Sales, marketing, and customer support members are all on the same team. It is critical to have honesty between each of these team members and to have alignment around goals. Utilizing a revenue team as well as daily revenue team standups is a tried and true way to ensure adequate communication and goal alignment between team members.
- There is never a shortage of things to do in a startup. While account-based marketing will

entail an investment of time in order to get up and running, it will save you time and effort in the long-run. It will allow you to concentrate on the most appealing type of customer and pursue them with all of your energy rather than focusing your efforts in a less-disciplined way. This focus will make the difference between success and failure.

Act I: Know Thyself

"To thine own self be true, and it must follow, as the night the day, thou canst not then be false to any man."
-- William Shakespeare

Every single person reading this book has the tools necessary to succeed in account-based marketing. I always get concerned when I see someone who is selling a dream of yet another marketing approach. The beauty of account-based marketing is that it's not another marketing approach; it is a fundamental truth. Rather than being about a system or philosophy, account-based marketing is all about focus. It is about rewarding the highest value work at each stage of the funnel.

If account-based marketing is a fundamental truth, then it follows that it requires you to be truthful with yourself and your company. I'm talking about brutal honesty, about avoiding the viewpoints that make us feel comfortable and instead asking the tough questions and answering them without bias. The echo chambers have got to be turned off and eradicated.

While we will cover three different acts in this book, Act 1, knowing yourself, is the most difficult. Act 1 isn't something they teach you in college or at business school. This is all about radical conversations. It is about seeing things as they actually are rather than as we wish they were. This applies to your own performance, your team's performance, and your company's performance.

In honesty lies all the marrow of marketing. If you are honest about where you are in the food chain, you can find your goals and the motivation to achieve them. While being honest about your shortcomings can be difficult, it gives you focus to know where you need to improve. Ultimately, this honesty is the first step towards building a world-class organization.

Step 1: To What Company are you (Really) Selling?

"Your competition is everything else your prospect could conceivably spend their money on." – **Don Cooper**

Let's take a look at a term I like to use: the ideal customer profile. The ideal means the highest average sales price in the shortest amount of time, with the lowest chance of churning. That sounds pretty straightforward, right? Who buys your software, likes your software, renews, and expands? Basic, right? But it's an overused term in some cases. Sometimes you walk into a room, and the ideal customer profile is anybody who is willing to write your company a check. While money is great and should feed your bonus pool, it's not the best way to sustainably grow a brand. If you only focus on selling indiscriminately, you will eventually exhaust your growth. I'll explain the reason behind this later.

There's usually a hyper-niche that you can fill. There's usually a particular type of company that does a particular type of thing that may be in a particular size for a particular occasion. Sometimes it comes down to something as simple as firmographic data, but that's not usually the whole story. Most importantly, the key to your company's hyper-niche is contained in your company's history. All you have to do is unlock it. Your company has experienced success, and there are answers to every success. You've just got to figure it out.

I'll tell you a quick story about my history. Some of the first successes that I shared earlier led to growth, and growth led to confidence. After a time, I began to think, "Hey, we can sell anybody this type of software!" Instead of maintaining our focus on the construction industry, we sold our software to a massive university. We justified the decision, believing the use cases to be similar enough. They did share many similarities, and it was easy to see how our software could help a school just as it had helped a construction company. Yet we overlooked that there were many differences as well. Despite their similarities, these two types of organizations were looking at the world through a different lens.

You know that little saying about touching the elephant? As the tale goes, the three blind men extend their hands to touch a giant elephant. One lays his hand on the elephant's leg, the other on the elephant's ear, and the third on the elephant's trunk. Each describes the elephant in completely different terms – each speaks the truth but has an entirely different understanding of the animal. Well, it was the same with these two types of companies, except more extreme: one organization described an elephant, and another described an apple orchard. There were no similarities. Perhaps an enormous company could divert its attention between two drastically different stakeholders, but there was no way a tiny startup could pull that off. So we made one of the toughest decisions we could at the time: instead of walking away from easy money and a new market as we should have done, we changed our company structure to heavily refocus on these large academic institutions. We weren't honest that these organizations didn't have a desperate need for our solution, and we weren't honest that our software didn't provide them with significant value.

Let me be clear: it didn't result in the apocalypse. Our revenue grew. It's easy to grow revenue when you expand to a new market... for a time. But as our new client base grew, our old customer base—our ideal customer profile—began to churn. Who do you really sell to? The answer is crucial to sustained growth. When it's all said and done, everybody is a hyper-niche marketer. It's just that only the winning companies know that they are indeed hyper-niche marketers.

Identifying your Ideal Customer Profile

Sometimes we've got to look at business-to-consumer (B2C) companies to learn. In many respects, B2C marketers are more advanced in marketing tactics. Typically, a B2C marketer analyzes their customer demographic. They are extremely thorough and consider every aspect of their customer profiles and personalities. They understand behavioral science because they're looking at data at scale. Some of the correlations they find are surprising. "Did you know that people who buy our stuffed animals also love Pabst Blue Ribbon? Who would have figured!" Take that concept and ask yourself, "Are we thinking that way?" The ideal customer profile has aspects that are firmographic. But understand that it isn't only firmographic data. I usually recommend starting this process on a Saturday. Take at least half a day to get the crucial conversation started between customer success, sales, and marketing leadership. Even invite your individual contributors. Sometimes they hold the best data.

Discuss firmographic data, but don't overly hang your hat on it. Sometimes your ideal customer profile doesn't actually behave in the same way. They may share character traits, they may read the same magazines, but they may not always have identical behavior. You'll have to dive a bit deeper. Cross-reference your assumptions with SAAS metrics for the companies that you think are your ideals. See how your ideal customer profile buys, how long it takes to close them, how often they churn, and what their average selling price is. And amidst all of this data, don't forget to trust your gut. This is art as much as it is science. What feels right, and what feels wrong? Ask yourself, for how many of these accounts can you pick up the phone today and ask for a reference? Randomly sample no less than one hundred accounts. If you only have fifty clients, sample all fifty of them. Keep reminding yourself that these are the people for whom you are looking. You are looking for patterns.

you are looking. You are looking for patterns. And those patterns are what's really going to help you focus down the road.

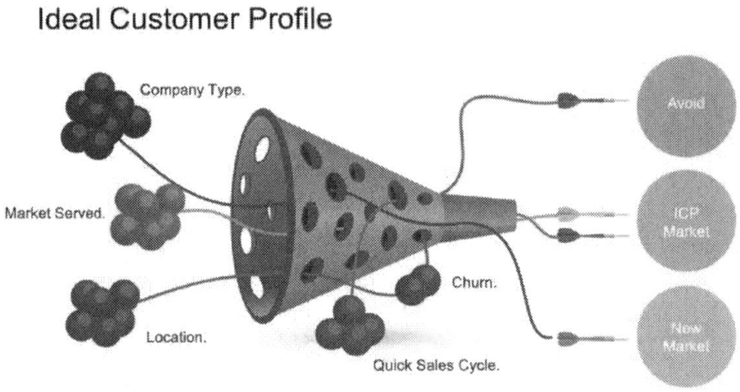

Ideal Customer Profile

Figure 1: The process of identifying your ideal customer profile

Exercise: Score your Clients

Take a moment amongst your revenue team to vote. It's a simple system. Ask yourself, of these one hundred clients, who is an "epicenter client"? Which client most represents your ideal? You get one point for that.

Next, vote for your "aftershock client," a client that is peripheral to the ideal. They are very similar to your ideal customer—they dress the same way but aren't growing quite perfect. There is a reason for this difference, and you need to figure it out. You can call this type of client an aftershock client, and you do not receive any points for them.

Finally, vote for your "earthquake clients," which are your poor match clients. These clients may have big, recognizable brand names, but they aren't a great fit for your solution. Often, they work in industries that don't make any sense for what you're doing. They may have paid a lot of money for your solution, but they don't love your product, and they don't advocate for your company. Typically, I've found that earthquake clients call customer support constantly. They complain, and quite frankly, they give you a bad reputation. You lose a point for each earthquake client.

Now that you have your three types of clients – your ideal customer profiles, your aftershock clients, and your earthquake clients – it's time to go through your entire client roster. For every ideal customer profile, you receive one point. For every aftershock client, you do not receive any points. And for every earthquake client, you deduct one point. Add all your points together and divide by the total number of your clients to find the average.

How did you do? If you end up with a score of 70% or higher, you are in the green. If you score between 50-70%, you are in the yellow. And if you are less than 50%, you are in the red. The goal is not to receive a high score. The goal is to be honest—brutally and vulnerably honest—with your team. If you're in the red, you can go back to the drawing board as a team and figure out what is going wrong. The only way to get into the green is by being honest and then systematically determining what changes need to be made.

The point of this exercise is to get better at identifying your ideal customer profile and finding ways to attract and retain them. This may involve "firing" your poor match clients. It's better to suffer the short-term revenue loss to free up resources to make your ideal customer profiles happier, as those are the ones that will grow your business.

Exercise: Score your customers

Figure 2 – Score your clients to gain clarity on your ideal customer profile

So far, we have talked about how to pinpoint the exact type of company with whom you would like to work. Remember my example of the construction magazine advertisements? The more you understand your ideal company, the more you will be able to quickly and effectively acquire more companies like them. But this is not just about companies. Ultimately, this boils down to people—the people at each company who help you become successful, and the people at each company who will try to crush your deal before it takes root. In the next chapter, we will delve deeper into understanding the types of people at each of your target companies.

Key Takeaways:
- Honesty—brutal honesty—will be crucial in helping your team and company grow. This honesty begins with being honest about what type of company you are selling. Not the type of company you wish you were selling to, or the type of company you hope you are selling to, but rather the type of company to whom you are actually selling.
- Once you know where you currently are, your next step is to figure out where you need to be. Developing an ideal customer profile is the first step towards navigating your way towards success. A clear, precise image of your best, most enjoyable, and most profitable type of customer will help you acquire more companies like them.
- Scoring your customers, while painful, is a valuable way for your team to gain clarity about which clients are helping you grow, which ones are not adding much value, and which customers are holding you back. While this process takes time, it will help you understand your ideal customer profile, your aftershock clients, and your earthquake clients.

Step 2: To What Company do you (Really) Sell?

"Make a customer, not a sale."
– Katherine Barchetti

Every team I have ever worked with loves to talk about the accounts to whom they sell. However, when all is said and done, you are in the business of selling to people, not accounts. Regardless of how great you are at identifying the accounts that should buy your software, it's even more vital that you can identify the people who are going to help close these deals.

So go to Salesforce (or whatever CRM system you're using) and run a Closed Won report. Start to look at all the conversations that occur on the way to a sale. There's always a door-opener, there's always a coach, there's always a person who signs the actual contract. And guess what? These key players are not alone. There are also a multitude of challenger personas. These challengers stand between you and a new client. They raise objections, they stall progress, and they prevent the deal from occurring.

You want to create the muscle memory of who to befriend and who to avoid. You want to become familiar with your allies, and know whom you need to win over. Identifying the right personas is not simply about titles or roles, although these are good starting points.

It may start with your team realizing, "Oh, the Chief Financial Officer was always a challenger in our deals!" If this is the case, you can start to prepare. You want to take this knowledge one step further. For example, perhaps you find that when the Chief Financial Officer comes from a large accounting firm, let's say one of the big three firms, and they have done an audit of your company, they tend to be allies in your deal. On the other hand, maybe you review your company data and realize that when the Chief Financial Officer has been with their company for 30 years, they typically didn't like your software. Similarly, you find that if a Chief Financial Officer received their CPA through night school, they also tend to become challengers to your software. All three of these stories are informing the type of person you should target (or avoid). Your ability to create vivid portraits of your target customer will make it significantly easier to go after the right person in each teal. This is behavioral analysis in action.

Building customer personas has become something of a fad in marketing. Personally, I hate personas that start off with "Jane the accountant" or "Bill the project manager." The reason why these names always annoy me is that who you are and the title you have are two exceptionally different characteristics. Let's be honest:

nobody is purely defined by their title. While we all have a primary title, especially in a growing startup, we will wear multiple hats at any one time. While titles help, they are only a partial view of the picture. Yet behavioral analysis is another thing entirely. It allows you to delve far past role into defining characteristics. There are great software resources available to help you narrow in on these behavioral characteristics. Far more than titles, these characteristics will give you a starting place from which to understand who needs to be part of your software deal.

To help with this process, I would recommend an exercise that I call the Persona Intercept Analysis. In any deal, there are intersecting levels of interactions. Where did the conversation begin? With whom did that initial person interact with after that? Did they need to get someone's opinion, to get someone else's approval, and yet someone else's buy-in for the deal? Which connections formed within the organization as a result of these conversations? When all was said and done, which people drove the deal through to completion?

Take a look at how those roles and persona profiles add up. Every Closed Won deal has a story. And every story has its own cast of characters. The Persona Intercept Analysis exercise is about getting to know each of these characters and understanding the overall narrative from the persona perspective. You might've met the IT person at a trade show during which they introduced you to a marketing executive. After a few conversations with the marketing executive, they mentioned that they needed to chat about this with an executive in the finance department.

this with an executive in the finance department. After that, they had to discuss this with someone from the Human Resources group. Meanwhile, someone from the sales department is in love with their current solution and started to oppose having to learn some new software system. Luckily, the operations team loved your product, and they championed the deal over the finish line.

Every deal has a story, and it's your job to follow the thread through all of the nooks and crannies of the organization to see where the deal went on its way to approval. These types of stories are what you need to understand what type of people make the deal happen. Remember that account-based marketing is simply marketing that is done really, really well.

Figure 3 – Using Persona Intercept Analysis to see which points of contact contribute to (and detract from) your success.

I'd also like to introduce the concept of a content supply chain. This is another exercise we will revisit later, but for now, think of it this way: as you develop each customer persona, continue to ask yourself "How can I best make this person aware of our solution? How do I increase our visibility within this company? How do I increase our visibility with the right people? How do I get them to trust me, my company, and our solution instead of just me as an individual? How do I become their trusted advisor? How do I equip them to close a deal for me?" Lastly, and quite possibly the most important, is to ask yourself "What do I need in order to get the deal done?"

I don't want to mislead you; this is a massive undertaking. However, even if this turns into a one or two-day project, this is an investment that will continue to pay dividends to you and your team. As we discussed before, honesty is essential in this process. If you combine honesty with the right data, and you'll set up a system that will bring about a transformational process in your company. You will start to identify the ideal companies to pursue and the right people to engage with those companies. Think of this as front-loading your work. Sometimes it takes time to save time, and this process is all about laying a solid foundation for your outreach. One of my favorite quotes is attributed to Abraham Lincoln, when he said, "Give me six hours to chop down a tree, and I will spend the first four sharpening the ax." If Abraham Lincoln was discussing account-based marketing, those first two-thirds of his time would be spent in identifying the most relevant players critical to a sales discussion.

So far, we have discussed how to get honest with your team about the ideal company. After that, we said that it's important to carry this one step further by taking a look at the exact person (or groups of people) to whom you are selling within these companies. At this point, you should feel confident that you at least have a hypothesis about your ideal customer profile. As valuable, you'll identify your anti-ideal company, the earthquake client. And you should have a sense of that in-between client, the aftershock client. These last ones are ok to take money from, but don't expect much of an expansion deal in the peripheral area.

The other aspect we considered in this chapter was how to target challengers, executioners, coaches, and door-openers. We're going to have the tools, or we're going to identify which tools we need, to do all of that. The next thing we will consider is why people are buying your software. There's a reason why people buy your software. I remember that on one Saturday, I've put up a bunch of post-it notes and said, "Why do they buy? Who buys us?" I started connecting strings between each post-it note, and my room quickly took on the appearance of a police department blotter! It may have looked insane, but it worked. So let's next consider why people are buying your software.

worked. So let's next consider why people are buying your software.

Key Takeaways:

- Account-based marketing is ultimately about people. While it is crucial to carefully identify the type of company you are pursuing, it is equally as vital to be explicit on the type of person within the organization with whom you need to interact. This goes beyond title into a behavioral analysis of the person's specific characteristics.
- Just as "it takes a village to raise a child," it also takes a village of people to close a sales deal. Start to identify the types of people involved in your sales process: challengers, executioners, coaches, and door-openers each play a part in your sales conversations. Become acquainted with each of these personalities so you can identify them (or avoid them) in advance.
- Persona Intercept Analysis and the Content Supply Chain are both exercises to help you refine your understanding of your ideal customer profile. While each of these takes additional time to analyze, understand, and explain to your team, they will ultimately be more efficient in growing your revenue as a result. Think of Abraham Lincoln sharpening his ax; in account-based marketing, it often takes time to save time.

Step 3: Why do People buy your Software?

"Most people think 'selling' is the same as 'talking'. But the most effective salespeople know that listening is the most important part of their job."
– Roy Bartell

While people's actions may seem irrational and unpredictable, there is always a reason behind the actions a person takes. Newton explained this succinctly in his Third Law: every action has an equal and opposite reaction. There is always a cause and effect. Buddhism calls this karma: the sum of a person's actions in this and previous states of existence decide their fate in future existences. Farmers know this better than most: you reap what you sow. So while it may seem that people are acting randomly, there is always some conditioning or underlying motive driving their actions.

The same principle applies to account-based marketing. Every single one of your customers purchased your software for a reason. It may not have been a good reason, and it may not be the reason you told them when you made the sale. Rest assured, though, that a reason does exist. Some customers may buy from you because you're the least expensive solution. Others may purchase from you because you have an exceptional reputation or

They heard about you from a trusted friend. Some customers may have seen the incredible brands you work with, and, aspiring to be like them, they want to use the same software as these legendary brands. Some customers may have just liked you as a person and wanted to help you out. As you might be tired of my saying, this is all about honesty. Let go of why you hope people buy from you or why you imagine they buy from you, and start to figure out the real reason behind their purchasing decisions.

There is a tremendous amount of ambiguity involved in building a company. To mitigate this, I have always found it helpful to create groupings of reasoning to reduce this ambiguity. When it comes to why customers buy, I reduce the various possibilities to just six "buckets" of reasons. Doing this will make your life simpler. Just as with understanding the types of people to whom you sell, you are building up muscle memory so that over time, you can more quickly identify the reason why a customer may buy from you.

Do they buy because you have features and benefits that nobody else has? Is there a uniqueness to your product? Do they buy to keep up with the Jones', or are they getting great referrals? Are we getting great referrals? Is there an advocacy program in place that's thriving? Is there a vision match? Do they dig where you're going? Maybe you believe you're reinventing an industry, and they want to reinvent it along with you. Is there a coolness factor? I tried on this in my last gig. Companies love the branded culture. They might want to partner with you to be perceived as a little cooler.

Do they love your deployment model? Or, let's be honest, were you the cheapest date at the dance? Maybe you have a lower cost of implementation and a higher level of service. Do you have an industry edge? Are you selling industry knowledge in a generic industry? Are you against generic software? Are you a good citizen of your industry? Ask yourself these questions. Put that on the board. You start drawing lines, finding out why your ideal customer profile buys your software, and you end up with a pretty good story.

Put more succinctly, these are the most common reasons I see for a customer's purchasing behavior:

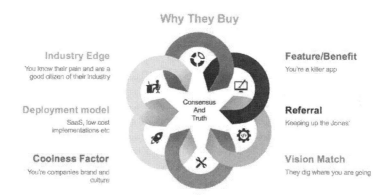

Figure 4 – The six most common reasons that customers purchase a product

At this point, we have discussed how to identify the accounts and companies that your team needs to target. We drilled in deeper and then covered how to identify the specific individuals at these companies that you need to find, as well as the ones who you need to identify. Then, we discussed how to determine the exact triggers that make these people want to buy from you. At this point, you've got yourself a platform that you can take to the next level. Now it's time to start talking about strategy, execution, and putting these principles to work.

Key Takeaways:
- While people's actions may seem random, rest assured: every customer has a reason why they buy from you (or a reason why they didn't purchase from you).
- This is not about guesswork; talk to your customers and uncover the primary reasons why they bought from you.
- While every customer is unique, the reasons they purchase from you will have overlap. The primary reasons customers buy software is for an Industry Edge, a Feature or Benefit, they come from a Referral, they have Vision Match with your company, they want your company's Coolness Factor, or they like your Deployment Model.

Act II: Strategy and Execution

"A rock pile ceases to be a rock pile the moment a single man contemplates it, bearing within him the image of a cathedral."
– Antoine de Saint-Exupery

Well, now we're starting to get into the fun stuff. The foundational elements of account-based marketing can actually be kind of boring and difficult, like eating your vegetables. The goal, though, is to be more agile and to be everywhere in the eyes of your target account. Now we have arrived at the point where the fun and creativity come into play. This is where you are going to start seeing the exponential growth in your revenue. In the following section, we're going to lay out the strategy for you to run with in order to start growing your company by leaps and bounds.

Before we start talking about execution, I do want to cover one very important factor: regardless of how accurate and refined your initial customer profile, you need to have a generic account plan for each permutation of your initial customer profile.

Here's what I mean by this: in the following chapters, we are going to talk about execution galore. We are going to cover multiple ways in which you can start growing your outreach and account list creatively. However, no matter how good you are at targeting ideal clients and getting meetings, you are still going to receive inbound inquiries from your ideal customer profile. For this reason, you're going to have to figure out how to get those deals done as well.

In the last section, we talked in great detail about identifying the highest value accounts for outreach. Before you even start targeting these accounts, you need to have real account plans in place. That means you need to understand the "who, when, and what" of each account, even before the account becomes a sales lead. Remember, these objectives will align your revenue team and increase your overall success and close rates for each account. A quick Google search yields a variety of pre-built templates that will help you delineate the "who, when and what" of each account. I would recommend that you spend a few minutes searching for a template that will work best for your team.

The other component of this section is the execution stage. Once you have these great accounts in Salesforce, you'll then need to go through the account discovery process. When you do this, I would recommend that you put on your marketing operations hat. Pretend that you are Columbus, and go searching for that new world of ideal customer profiles. LinkedIn is fantastic for this purpose. If you have a crisp sense of what your ideal customer profile is, you can use LinkedIn's Sales Navigator to quickly and efficiently narrow in on these types of people.

people. You can refine your search by geographic area, title, company size, revenue size, seniority level…there are so many different criteria to help you more effectively leverage your ideal customer profiles. Whether or not you use LinkedIn, do whatever you have to so that you can start to create a list of people matching your ideal customer profile. Here is where all that hard work pays off; finally, you're able to cleanly sort through tens of thousands of companies and individuals and hone in on the needle in the haystack.

Before we move on to this section, I also wanted to set a distinction between the account-based marketing funnel and the traditional sales funnel. The traditional funnel is antiquated and outdated. I refer to it with my teams as the "hopes and dreams funnel." You hope somebody downloads your e-book. You hope they give you a real email address. You hope they give you their phone number and actual name, rather than a bogus name and email. You hope and you dream all day long. And more often than not, these hopes and dreams don't get you very far. They certainly don't get you to the exponential growth you're craving. The "hopes and dreams funnel" is usually associated with another buzz word: lead velocity. It is mindboggling to think that you are paying for every one of these leads, yet most of them are total garbage. Nonetheless, this is the traditional funnel that B2B marketers have dealt with for years.

This path is well-trodden: start by getting a bunch of leads. These leads become a bunch of prospects, and these prospects become a pipeline. Hopefully, this bunch of pipeline becomes a hefty portion of Closed Won opportunities. If you're lucky, you achieve a high Close Rate, and the resulting Closed Won list is fairly respectable. On the other hand, if you are unlucky, you are going out of business. C'est la vie. This is not a good way to use money in marketing sales for customer success. Quite frankly, this path is in the age of the dinosaurs when it comes to marketing.

Understanding the ABM funnel

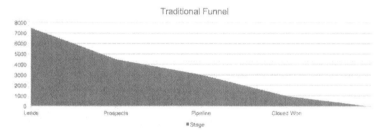

Figure 5 – A depiction of the traditional "hopes and dreams funnel"

Instead of the "hopes and dreams funnel," this is what the account-based marketing funnel should look like:

ABM funnel

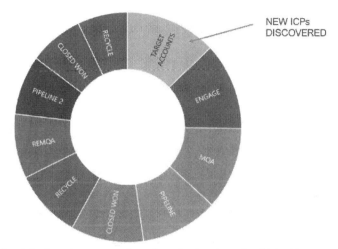

Figure 6 – A look at the account-based marketing funnel, which allows
you to rinse and repeat your approach as a continual process.

Above is what an ABM funnel should look like. You
start off with target accounts at the top of the wheel.
These are accompanied by ideal customer profiles
which are discovered through other lead-gen means.
Together, we engage these leads. We engage them
constantly, and we engage them relentlessly.

Use a calculation to say, "Hey, this account is
warmed up, or not. It's marketing qualified." Based on
this objective classification, accounts become part of
the pipeline. If they convert, they become a Closed
Won client. If they don't convert, no worries; we
engage them again and repeat the process. We recycle
these

unconverted leads and continue the cycle. It's a new funnel where you can continuously rinse and repeat. It's much saner, and it's far more ordered. It gives you full-funnel metrics without the craziness of creating a bunch of garbage leads.

You are always going to be finding your new ideal customer profile. If you're reading this and you're a believer that the only way to grow your company is to hire a bunch of 20-year-old kids to make outbound phone calls…well, I'm not sure I can help you. Instead, I would recommend that you subscribe to an alternative viewpoint. Rather than having your Business Development Representatives assigned to inbound and outbound activities, I would suggest you reassign them to either assigned or unassigned activities. If a lead is not yet ready to buy, they are unassigned leads, and they receive attention and engagement. When they are ready to talk, they go into an assigned mode in which you can attempt to close them. If they're not yet ready, they can go back to the unassigned grouping.

Marketing needs to change as well. Wide swath demand generation will always have to happen. But your goal is to start making sure that an engagement is an engagement with an ideal customer profile. What if you're not sure if the account is an ideal customer profile? Well, then you need to go out and get more information and more data about that account. It's simple: if you don't have enough context, get more context.

When sales and marketing both take this approach, not only does the company win, but I can guarantee that your customer success team will be a lot happier as well. Rather than spending time corralling a whole menagerie of customers, they'll be able to focus all of their attention on the customers with whom your company should be working. This will lead to increased customer retention, increased referrals, and increased happiness for your customer success team.

Now that we have the basis for understanding our approach to strategy and execution, let's examine something you may think is only for developers. Let's start by talking about agile planning.

Key Takeaways:
- Marketing is changing and the traditional "hopes and dreams funnel" is not going to get you where you want to go. Instead, approach the account-based marketing funnel as a continuous wheel of engagement.
- Align your sales and marketing team, so that they can approach a lead as either assigned or unassigned.
  If the lead isn't ready to purchase, that's not a problem. Add them back to the process, rinse, and repeat.

Step 4: Agile Planning

"In preparing for battle I have always found that plans are useless, but planning is indispensable."
-- Dwight D. Eisenhower.

Agile planning isn't just for developers; it's just as important for marketers. Unfortunately, many people view agile planning as chaotic. It is a very different approach to marketing, but it is far from chaos. The truth is that if you have members of your team that cannot keep up with the rapid pace of agile planning, you'll be doing a big favor to yourself, them, and your team if you show these members the door.

Agile planning is about experimentation. Start with an experimental budget and a hypothesis. What is the most effective way to attract more of your ideal customer profiles? Once you've got your budget in place and your plan delineated, it's time to lace up your team's shoelaces and get ready to sprint.

At agile planning's core is a foundation of two-week sprints. It is about taking the time to set your priorities and to set your direction, and then strapping on a jet-pack to get there in a hurry. Ultimately, agile planning is about a race to zero…zero cost per lead. You want to use the short duration of two weeks to exploit every opportunity to acquire new ICP leads. You want to absolutely own your marketing channels. You want to be on every channel simultaneously. Throughout the sprint, you want to be hyper-focused on your primary engagement goal, which is list-building. Your only two objectives are to find more ideal customer profiles (or obtain more information about these ICPs), followed by getting more revenue. Those are the only two goals you have got.

Let me be clear: when I say "Own the channel," I mean that you have to completely and utterly own the channel. You need to own it all. When I say, "Race to a zero cost per lead," I mean that the goal is not to have the highest marketing budget in the world. You want to win the title of the most efficient marketing budget in the world.

Agile marketing entails analyzing your marketing data so as not to over-commit on your annual budget. I find it astounding how much marketing budgets have grown in the last decade. When I started out in marketing, I had to know exactly what campaigns I was going to run one year before I would run them, and I needed an extraordinary amount of specificity. This approach is the opposite of agile planning, but it forced me to be disciplined. It forced my team to look at the data and aim...aim again...aim again...and aim one more time before we pulled the trigger on any marketing activity.

Of course, things change over time, and we would invariably see topics come up that we hadn't anticipated. We often saw that the ROI differed from what we had anticipated. There are always so many different variables: products get delayed, key clients are won, and a multitude of different factors all interrupt your perfect waterfall marketing plans. Yes, there are things that you can predict, such as wide net marketing activities like Google Ad Words. In cases like this, you can plan your monthly marketing budget and stick to it with a reasonable amount of certainty. But again, account-based marketing involves focusing on very niche approaches.

In subsequent chapters, we will explore tactics including emails, displays, webinars, and customs. Each of these tactics is associated with a high degree of variance that will make it difficult, if not impossible, to commit to a budget or target number far in advance. In the spirit of honesty, agile planning is being honest that you do not have a crystal ball and you cannot predict events far into the future. It limits the future to two weeks, which is much more manageable and allows you to be far nimbler. This is why agile planning becomes so powerful and important.

Here is an example of how you can set up your organization to master agile planning:

1. Put a team together that consists of a content producer, a creative, a digital marketing expert and brand or idea person. I call these groupings of team members a Squad.
2. Work with your Product Marketing team (or, if you do not yet have a product marketing team, work directly with your Product or Research & Development team) to discover the touch points that should resonate with your target accounts. Including competitive takeouts; do your target accounts run a specific tech

stack that you can replace? You should also look at the features and functions that are essential before go to market. Competitive takeouts may also include timely topics that are on the horizon, such as changes in legislation that affect your market. Using this plan, you can create Epics, which are simply groupings of different sprints that relate to each other.

3. Plan your first sprint. Put the pieces together and start sending emails, update your targeted display ads, and use anything you can from the tools described in subsequent steps.

4. Have a strong feedback loop. Remember that you are targeting specific ICPs, which should be converting to inbound engagements. If you do not see these ICPs turning into demos and opportunities, you need to be able to identify this and refine your approach quickly.

5. Include your sales team in your feedback loops. Since the sales team is responsible for classifying a lead as an engagement, it is important that they are involved in your feedback loop. It is a good idea to make sure the sales team knows what is coming next and what the talk tracks should be. For example, if you have an Epic on a specific go-to market strategy, your sales representative needs to know the talk track for the specific features you are promoting as well as the reasons why these features will have a massive impact on your ICP. If your sales reps don't understand this, your entire Epic is a waste. Never break the value chain. This means that your marketing team needs to present to your sales team, so the

sales reps understand your goals and the way in which they must speak target accounts.

Now the marketing machine transforms from a quiet, pretty-pictures department to a roaring machine. Trust me: you will hear lots of cheers, laughter, and chatter. Your team will love riding the waves of success, and they will be impacted by the sprints and tactics that don't work. But marketing will be fun again. Instead of hiding behind annual, this strategy of waterfall-planning marketing is on the field, operating and directly impacting the uptick in revenue.

The challenges are significant—agile planning can feel like a hamster wheel. Really. It can be stressful and makes the marketers think 24/7. Home and work blend together. There are always lots of balls in the air, lots of moving parts. Quite frankly, you can burn out your team a lot. But that can be offset with some really important learning moments, and most importantly by variable compensation that is based on the revenue success. This is a different type of marketing, but when implemented correctly, it is a huge step forward.

Now that your team has a roadmap to start using agile planning (as well as a plan to get rid of the team members who can't handle this pace), our next step is to figure out your company's story.

Key takeaways:

- Agile planning is not just for developers. It is a critical element of high-performing marketing teams. If a member of your team cannot keep up with the pace of agile planning, it is best to move them on sooner rather than later.
- Agile planning allows you to experiment as rapidly and efficiently as possible, with the goal of achieving a customer acquisition cost of zero. Your goal should be to become the world's most efficient marketing team, not the marketing team with the largest budget.

Step 5: What's the Story?

"The stories we tell make the world. If you want to change the world, you need to change your story. This truth applies both to individuals and institutions."
--Michael Margolis

What's the story? A company needs to be like a chat-bot: pose a question, and everybody should say the same thing. In a world where everyone is considered unique, I know this may not be a popular answer, but it's true. There are common questions that every member of your team will be asked, and you, as a team, need to have an aligned message. How was this company founded? Every single member of your company better have this inspiring and heartfelt story down cold. What makes a great client? Whether you're in sales, marketing, customer success, or even development, you should be able to describe this client as if it were your first true love. Being able to tell stories consistently is never easy, and it's a never-finished process. But it is always essential, and it is always a work in progress.

Stories are the most efficient way to transmit information in a way that will allow the listener to retain your message. We are a species of storytellers. Our ancestors shared stories around the campfire and imparted messages of survival and cultural norms. We inherently tune in to the emotional overtones of a story, and these reside in our memory long after we've forgotten facts and figures. We grew up as children hearing parables, fables, and stories. It is hardwired into who we are.

This fact provides a significant advantage to your team. If they can consistently tell stories to customers, your company will stand out. Each member of your team should have a handful of success stories about the clients who love you most. If a potential customer asks for a feature, be ready to share the customer feedback you received that caused you to build that feature. If the potential customer has a concern about your software, be ready to share the story of another customer who had a similar concern but was blown away by how your system performed. These stories underlie your company's value and also use social proof to illustrate that others trust you.

The storytelling process is not easy, and it's always a work in progress. If you operate in a set of industries, be a citizen of that industry. Know what is happening in that industry. Love your industry and embrace it as if it were your college fraternity. Take the time to craft and practice an actual narrative around your company's most salient points. What is the story of your company? Why are things the way they are? If you have a sales rep that can't tell those stories after you explain it to them on a constant basis, they need to move on.

Avoid words like "modernizing" or other vague terms. You know the words; they've been used too often on every deck, and are plastered all over your competitor's website. Be specific, unique, and easily understandable.

Remember that there are phases of engagement with your potential customers. Here, again, is the content supply chain:

Have a clear plan for what you are trying to communicate at each stage. Don't focus on trying to cram every last benefit down your prospect's throat in your first interaction. Pace yourself. Stick to one simple message for each stage in their journey, and stick with each stage's most important aspect. For example, if the prospect doesn't know who you are, make sure they not only understand who you are but that they never forget you. Create awareness. If the prospect does know who you are, build up trust so that you are a confidante and friend. Give them social proof and customer stories that foster trust. If you view yourself as a citizen of your industry, you can further aim to become an ambassador and leader within your industry.

Once the prospect starts to trust you, give them the information that you can use to teach them how to be a better company by using your software as one of their tools, not the only tool. Be their coach. Think about how you can help them succeed in their role and in their industry. If they are successful, you will be successful, and they will know that you are on their side. Because you know why they buy, solve their problems and get the biggest deal you can get.

We have already considered the agile planning process, which is essential to help determine your most efficient channel for marketing. Once you determine an efficient way to get in front of your customers, the next step is to find the most efficient way to transmit information through concise and compelling stories. Now that we know both of these aspects of marketing, it's time to talk about something you may not be expecting: email and why it is still alive and well.

Key takeaways:
- We are a species of storytellers. We recall information that is transmitted to us through a compelling narrative faster and with more emotion.
- It takes time and energy to craft a compelling story around the most frequently-asked questions. It takes even more effort to teach these stories to your team in a way that will allow them to share them with customers and potential customers authentically. If you can do both of these, your company will be memorable and stand out from amongst the competition.

Step 6: Email is Alive and Well

"I do love email. Wherever possible, I try to communicate asynchronously. I'm really good at email."
-- Elon Musk

Email is alive and well, so please, for the love of all that is holy, stop sending newsletters. Nobody wants your newsletters. They don't. Nobody wants your poorly written blog posts gathered together in a tired newsletter template. Instead of focusing on newsletters, focus on nurturing. Creating an intelligent nurturing system requires metrics and an understanding that this is all about human behavior. What is it that your potential customer needs to learn at each point in their journey? If you are hyper-focused on what the customer needs, you'll realize that it's not always about the sale; it's often about giving the customer the information they need to succeed in their job today. Sometimes it's about giving them a distraction and a funny article. It's always about understanding what they need in each moment and doing your best to provide exactly that.

I'd like to share a quick story. A few years ago, I released a new product to an entirely new customer segment, a product that also required an entirely new role. I thought I had a home run on my hands. The product was related to safety, and I believed we were releasing this product at the perfect time for those interested in safety; I figured that safety managers would be all over this product and it would be flying off our shelves. But you have to remember that behavior tells you everything. After looking at customer behavior, we started to realize that it was actually the Finance Department personnel who were most interested in our safety product. The Safety Managers, as it turned out, were so busy and overwhelmed doing safety management work that they wouldn't notice our product if it knocked on their front door. Realizing that we had this unexpected audience, we modified our emails to appeal to the Finance Department and used terms and stories that resonated with that group of people.

Email works for B2B marketing, so long as you send items that are valuable to your recipients.. Given how many emails people receive today, you need to stand out and be bold. If you sound just like everyone else, your emails will never get any visibility.

Here's an example of what this might look like:

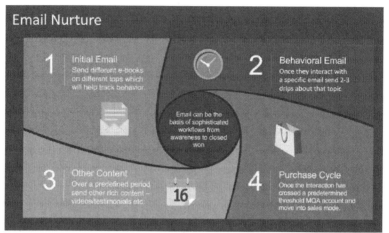

Figure 7 – An example of a group of emails designed to deliver the most value to your customer based on where they are in their discovery cycle.

News you can use

One great tactic I implemented at a previous company was to create a news website. Yes, we created a legitimate news website and recruited journalists across the nation to report on news that we felt our target accounts and personas would care about. The news crossed well beyond our product categories. It included everything from healthcare to mental health to career advice. We even got partner companies to expand on that information with their own articles. We had high-powered, persona-based interviews. We even provided a platform for our clients' own PR news engine so that they could market their own brand in a unique way. We went so far as to develop an industry health metric that people could use to check the stock market so that they could see how their industry was doing. We grew from 0 subscribers to over 300,000 in under three months. The reason why it worked so well was that we focused on real news. This was not an annoying little blog. Our emails about the new site received incredible open rates and responses, and they drove even more engagement. Remember, the resulting behavior is more important than saying, "Hey, buy my software." From this effort, we learned what subscribers were interested in, what they read the most, and why they cared about the subject. This data is more important than anything else; looking at client interaction with news gave us massive information for new email topics and nurtures!

Up until this point we've talked about your agile planning, and we've covered how to craft unified stories across your company. We have also chatted about email marketing and how this is still relevant today for both B2C and B2B marketing. Let's take things even one step further and talk about direct mail.

Key takeaways:
- It's not about newsletters; it's about quality nurturing. If you know your ideal customer profile, you'll understand what they need at every step of their journey. Utilize email to provide value to customers, and you will stand out amongst the competition.
- Your message can be perfect, but what matters most is who receives the message. Make sure you are sending your emails to the appropriate person—it

may be the department or individual you
least expect.

Step 7: Direct Mail

If you were surprised that I said that email is alive and well, then I'll bet you passed out when I said I was going to talk about direct mail. I love direct mail because it merges old school and new school into something powerful. If you are looking to build a lasting workflow that will nurture your customer, there is no shortage of tools out there to help you. However, of all the tools that I have used, direct mail has been my preeminent choice.

Direct mail offers an amazing toolset. Let me give you an example from a few years ago. My marketing team and I were assembled for our agile planning session. We were gaining momentum in the marketplace, but we didn't want to rest on our laurels. We needed to find a way to break through all the noise and stand out from our competition for good. I worked hard to maintain an environment in which every member of our team, from the most junior to the most senior, had respect and a valued perspective. While this can be challenging at times, if you are seriously committed to it, your team will gain confidence and will start to share incredible (though sometimes outlandish) ideas. My work paid off when one of our junior Business Development Representatives dared to propose a crazy idea: let's send video messages to our customers…by mail. "By email?" someone corrected.

Nope—by snail mail. Picture a rottweiler with a hotdog delicately balanced on his nose, just waiting for his master's command before he gobbles it up. That's how it felt at the time: as though this poor young BDR was about to be laughed out of the room. Instead, we thought about his suggestion and heard him out. I'm grateful we did.

Although none of us realized it, there was an inexpensive technology that allowed you to embed a miniature TV screen inside a greeting card. You could record up to a 60-second video that would play when the card was opened. Agile is all about experiments, and this would be one doozy of an experiment. So we had the BDR sit down and record a video in which he picked up the phone, looked at the camera, and said, "My name is Ryan, and I'm going to be calling you about my company, Procore. I hope you pick up, because I'd love to speak with you." We sat down every one of our BDRs and had them record a similar message. Then we matched the mailing list to each of the BDR's call lists so that they would, in fact, be able to call the person who received their recorded video message.

As I'm sure you've guessed at this point, we had an unbelievable response rate. That unbelievable response rate converted into an unparalleled pipeline. And that unparalleled pipeline turned into a record-making amount of Closed Won revenue. Once a prospect received the video card, the average response rate to the BDR's first phone call was over 61%! In the world of sales outreach, this is the equivalent of winning the lottery three weeks in a row and then getting struck by lightning. 61% response rates do not happen in today's marketing environment, but this outlandish idea achieved the seemingly impossible. Those 61% response rates turned into $7M of pipeline generated, which converted into $1.9M in Closed Won deals. Not bad for an idea that was hatched at an agile planning session, right?

I like to use this story to illustrate that direct mail is your gateway into targeted conversations. For our team, it didn't stop with TV video greeting cards; that was just the beginning. At this point, I have done it all. I've sent View-Masters that allowed the prospect to flip through different photos which introduced a BRD and our company. I've sent actual shoes and notes saying that we would do whatever it took to get our shoe in the door with this client. I have taken a wide array of approaches, each more unexpected than the previous.

However, there's one thing that I have never done, and that is sending booze. Alcohol is lazy marketing. I have been the recipient of booze countless times, and let me tell you that every time I receive alcohol by direct mail, they send me the wrong booze! I do what 99% of people do—I end up giving it away and completely forgetting about the company that sent it.

Direct mail provides your opportunity to get creative. I recommend that you never send more than one-hundred pieces of mail at one time. I also recommend that you never spend more than thirty dollars per piece of direct mail. If you follow my recommendations, that's only $3,000. That's not a lot of money, and I would argue that most companies can afford that. Try it, and you will see the results. Make sure that you are creative in your approach, and make sure that your direct mail is part of an overall cadence of nurturing (which could include email, phone calls, events, or other conversations).

Now that we have discussed email and direct mail, let's take things one step more personal and talk about trade shows.

Key Takeaways:
- Direct mail, when used creatively and as part of a broader nurture strategy, has by far been my most successful channel for outreach.
- While you can send just about anything by direct mail, avoid sending alcohol; it is a lazy approach that lacks the creativity and finesse of other alternatives.
- You don't have to break the bank to try direct mail and see the impact. You can keep the expenditure under $3,000 and see tenfold the revenue. Make sure you have other nurture touchpoints to support this effort.
- Be authentic in your approach. Outlandish is okay, but make sure it aligns with your message and who you are as a company.

Step 8: Own a Tradeshow

If a given trade show isn't pre-planned at the level of the Normandy Invasion, it's doomed to fail. Sales meetings need to be pre-scheduled, speaking slots secured, and every show attendee assigned specific objectives—from thoroughly deconstructing a competitor's pitch to making a number of new contacts."

– Simplilearn CMO, Mark Moran

Own a trade show. A lot of people out there think that trade shows don't work. They do. Trade shows offer one big advantage: you know that most of your targeted individuals are going to be there at one time. It's almost like stalking, I know. But at the end of the day, that's what a trade show delivers. They bring out the people that you want to talk to at your target accounts. Just take everybody else that you meet there as gravy, the icing on the cake of trade shows.

Hotel room drops are a great way of getting those folks' attention. Sometimes hotels don't like it when marketers do this, but if the conference is hosted through a hotel, hotel drops can work wonders, just like direct mail. For example, you could send a cheese plate to a prospect's room along with a handwritten card inviting them to meet you at your conference booth. Think Valentine's Day, but for your ICP instead of your spouse.

Given how many of your ICPs will be at a trade show, it is also an ideal time to host a dinner. You can single out your most important prospects, treat them to dinner, and get to know them in a much more intimate setting than the traditional phone call or conference room meeting. These actions can help you forge lasting relationships, and I've sometimes seen such relationships continue onward for decades. If you want to add even more value, host a dinner with a speaker. Make sure you choose your speaker well so that every prospect who attends will not only walk away with a full stomach but also with a handful of ideas to help them succeed.

One of the most important things to remember in preparation for trade shows is that you must be aligned with your account reps. Reps have one purpose at a trade show: badge-hunt. I've seen many companies make the fatal mistake of using their account reps to work their company's booth at trade shows. This is such a missed opportunity! While your goal may be to get people to your booth or to dinner, this is a team effort. Therefore, you need to figure out exactly who you want to meet at the trade show before the event even begins. LinkedIn can make your planning more effective by allowing your reps to get acquainted with the person's face in addition to their name. Once your reps have this "targeted hit list" of people, unleash them at the trade show. They need to scour the floor in search of these high-value prospects. I always like to make this into a game. If each rep has a list of 50 targeted people, start keeping score. How many of these leads are they able to find and convince to come to your booth or event? Never underestimate the power of success metrics to motivate your team and make for some fun and friendly competition.

If your team can work together on this, it will have a transformational effect. Your reps will hunt to bring the best prospects to your booth. Once these prospects are at your booth, it's story time. Now is when all of that time your team spent practicing their stories pays off. You're able to capture these leads and tell them stories of customer success and share the story of why your company is going to be the industry leader. One of the reasons I love to bring along new team members to a trade show is for practice. In an hour of operating a booth, the new team members will give their sales pitch hundreds, if not thousands, of times. Talk about trial by fire! By the end of their first few hours, they will be battle-tested. They will get very direct feedback from each prospects reaction, questions, and interest level about what words are working, what stories are resonating, and what benefits most interest them.

This is also your chance to get to know your potential customers face-to-face. You'll be able to learn what their biggest pain points are and how you can make their lives easier. While market research is essential, this added qualitative side is just as vital. This is your chance to build that empathy muscle. What keeps your customers up at night? What are they thinking of next? What have they seen at the trade show that is most impressive?

Soak up as much knowledge and understanding as you can.

The final piece of this process is the follow-up. No matter how great the conversation at your booth or dinner, you need to remember that trade shows are whirlwinds. You may spend thirty minutes getting to know a prospect and establishing a quality bond. However, that is one of literally hundreds of such conversations that prospect will have at the trade show. One thing that has helped me is to take notes on each person's business card. As soon as the person leaves my booth, rather than engaging the next prospect (which is tempting!), I take thirty seconds to write a summary of the conversation. What was her dog's name? What was her biggest pain point? What was the most memorable part of the conversation? Later that day or week when I follow-up, I've now got some notes to jog my memory and help me stand out from the rest.

We should also consider the opposite end of the spectrum. If trade shows are widely-held events that gather many of your ICP's, let's talk about the direct mail equivalent: simple custom events.

Key takeaways:
- Trade shows and events are like shooting fish in a barrel—many of your ICP's will be in one place at the same time. Take advantage of this by doing your homework in advance. Know exactly who you want to speak to and use your account reps to find them and bring them to your dinner or booth.

- Hotel room drops with personal invitations or hosted dinners with speakers are great ways to stand out, add more value to your potential customer, and get to know them in a more personal way.
- Without proper follow-ups, the entire trade show is a waste. Take notes about each quality conversation so that you can prioritize your follow-ups and jog the person's memory about who you were. Given how many conversations occur at each trade show, you need to be memorable and stand out from the rest.

Step 9: Simple Custom Events

"Before everything else, getting ready is the secret of success."

– Henry Ford

I've run some great user conferences and roadshows. 100 people showed up at my first user conference, but by the time I was done, I had grown this to over 2,000 people. Along the way, I kept track of what worked and what fell flat, and I implemented field marketing.

Field marketing is the black belt level of account-based marketing. Although I have used field marketing in the B2B space, it is actually a concept that I co-opted from the B2C space. To better understand this, think of the Red Bull model, or the Pepsi Taste Challenge. In each of these cases, the company hosted an epic event. Such events are filled with industry leaders and respected personalities. These leaders and personalities attend the event and also talk about your company. If you're Red Bull, these people could be extreme athletes. If you're IBM, they could be respected PhDs in your field. The point is to find the most influential people in your space and get them on your side.

Dinners are quite possibly the simplest way to get started with simple custom events. Make them entertaining and fun; think of the type of dinner party you would want to attend with your friends, and use that as the starting point. Let the dinner group get to know each other and become comfortable. Sure, a few bottles of wine always help with this, but you can do better than that. What's a way for each person to introduce themselves? Go past the "what do you do for a living?" part of the conversation, and think "Cards Against Humanity" rather than Dinner Etiquette 101. What's one of their most embarrassing moments growing up? What's the best vacation they've ever had? What's their favorite New Year's Eve memory? Getting the members of a dinner party comfortable with each other will unlock more meaningful conversations as the night goes on.

The composition of the dinner group plays an important role as well. I have always aimed to keep the group size to ten people or less. This allows for the entire group to be engaged in a conversation without anyone being left out. Make sure you have variety of people in your group—you want as many diverse perspectives as possible. Think through thought-provoking questions that you can ask the group. Your role is to keep the conversation moving and to drive towards actionable insights. You want your guests walking way thinking about how much they learned from the dinner conversation. And you want them to associate your company with these sorts of quality insights.

It doesn't have to be dinner. I've taken simple custom events on the road and have done everything from a very quick luncheon to a major user conference that attracted international attendees. You decide, but remember, the reason that you're running these custom events is that you want to talk to your target.

We did over one hundred events a year at my company. One of the things that helped us in each of these events was to own the message. Just as we learned with storytelling, we planned out the top three messages we wanted to impart at each event. We then worked to align every speaker, question, backdrop, and guest with these top three messages. The bigger the event, the easier it is to have your message diluted. This approach to planning can keep your team aligned and avoid a muddled event experience.

Another thing I've learned from hosting hundreds of simple custom events is to go to one of two extremes: either do the event on an extreme budget or go all out. I have done events that lie in between those two extremes, but they are not nearly as effective. I have hosted exceptional and memorable events that people talked about for years, and that were put together on a shoestring budget. I've also hosted events that cost more than some company's annual marketing budget. Both of these have their place, and both can be effective—you need to decide upfront what you want your event to be. When planning simple custom events, there is a tendency for costs to expand quickly. Before you know it, your event costs you one-hundred times what you had budgeted. From the outset, decide whether you're going the cheap route or the extravagant route, and then go all-in in that direction.

It can be fun to string these simple custom events together. One year, we strung together dozens of events: dinners, drinks, and luncheons that took us all the way to an event at Nascar. At times, I felt like a rock star on an around-the-world tour. By the time we got to our final event, we were all exhausted. But we had many repeat customers at events; it felt like we got in a lifetime of bonding with them over just a few weeks. I always like to encourage people to think about how they may group these events to lead to one final, culminating blow-out.

Now that we've talked about the in-person and intimate atmosphere that is found at both trade shows and simple custom events, let's go online. We should also consider the power of webinars and how best to use them.

Key takeaways:
- Simple custom events can be everything from an extravagant dinner party to a simple luncheon. Set your budget upfront and choose whether you're going to do it on the cheap or go all out.
- The composition of the group is crucial to getting a lively and insightful discussion. How you introduce the group (and the size of the group) are the foundational steps that will help the group memorably connect with each other.
- Consider stringing together events in a way that builds towards a grand finale. You'll create lasting bonds that will convert to a massive pipeline.

Step 10: Webinars for One

"The most important principle for designing lively eLearning is to see eLearning design not as information design but as designing an experience."
—Cathy Moore

Webinars are one of my favorite topics. In my career, I have led webinars on topics that are so specific and so niche that it seems absurd. However, the more specific the webinar, the better I have found the results. For example, "Hey, have you recently won an airport job in the Pacific Northwest? If so, you got to catch this webinar!" While this topic may seem so absurdly niche, it is the webinar you would want to attend if you had just won a contract with the Portland Airport. And guess what? We did our research and found this to be true to one of our ICPs, so we created a webinar just for them. It worked! They dialed in, and we eventually won the deal.

When you are hosting a webinar with the intended audience of one, it's obviously important that you hide the number of attendees in the room. While you may have constructed the webinar for just one person, you don't want them to feel like they're the only one there. That's the beauty of a webinar: many people will be unwilling to jump on a sales call where they are singled out, but they will join a webinar during their lunch break. So while it is just the same as a private sales call, the webinar format makes it feel more accessible for many people.

Many times, I will even queue up stock questions. During the presentation, I will pause and announce the question to the group and then provide the answer. While it may feel awkward, it does manage to break up the presentation as well as deliver information differently.

If you understand what your ideal customer profile wants, you'll understand the type of information that would most help them. Your goal, then, is to do the research, to do the heavy lifting to create a presentation that is an irresistible offer for your ICP. Once you have the presentation built, you can start to do targeted outreach. Because your presentation is so unique, it is highly likely to capture your ICP's attention.

While this is a lot of work, don't lose heart while compiling your presentation. Again, with account-based marketing it takes time to save time. Know that the odds are incredibly high that you will have a meeting shortly after your webinar.

At this point, we have looked at using agile planning to accelerate towards zero cost of customer acquisition. We have considered how your team can utilize email, direct mail, tradeshows, custom events, and even webinars to engage with your core audience. Now, we are going to shift directions talk about how important it is to surround all of the key players within an account. We'll discuss how marketing doesn't stop at the pipeline.

Key takeaways:
- Webinars for one are my favorite tool. They represent the epitome of being absolutely absorbed with your ICP. This approach takes an unbelievable amount of effort, as you have to understand what your ICP needs to know and create a presentation that is likely to be seen by only one ICP. But this juice is worth the squeeze. It will yield more meetings with more excited prospects than you have ever seen before.

Act III: Crush it!

"Everyone wants to live on top of the mountain, but all the happiness and growth occurs while you're climbing it."
— Andy Rooney

Be creative, that's all I got to say. If you've done it all right, Act III is all about crushing it. Everything that we have discussed up until this point has laid the foundation so that you can get your company into your sweet spot and completely dominate.

Years ago, Joel Peterson said something that I will never forget. Joel is a professor at the Stanford Graduate School of Business, the Chairman of the Board of Directors for Jet Blue Airlines, and one of the most impressive business operators I have ever met. What Joel said was: "You will earn the majority of your wealth between ages forty and fifty. Everything that you do in your career is simply building you up to the point so that when you are at this age, you can crush it."

This book, so far, has hopped from foundational lily pad to foundational lily pad. At this point, you have all the basics you need. For that reason, in this final section, we'll discuss the last elements necessary to crush it. We'll talk about the specific skills and mindsets you'll need to grow your market share.

Step 11: Marketing Doesn't Stop at the Pipeline

"A brand for a company is like a reputation for a person. You earn reputation by trying to do hard things well."
— **Jeff Bezos**

Marketing does not stop at the pipeline. Understand that. I'll give you an example. There are a lot of great accounting software companies that provide expense-tracking software for accounting teams. One day, while I was grabbing coffee in the morning, I saw one of these accounting software companies in our conference room. This wasn't anything new—I was well accustomed to seeing companies like this pitching our accounting team. What caused me to pause, instead, was that the conference room was filled with our sales representatives. There wasn't a single accounting person in the conference room. What was going on? I went into the conference room, and I saw that the expense approval software company was in full-blown sales mode, showing all the ins and outs of how easy it was to get an expense claim approved. They were giving the full dog and pony show, but I had no idea why they were bothering to do this with the sales representatives.

The conference room table was full of snacks, cookies, and other treats. *Well,* I thought, *at least the sales team is getting something out of this.*

Within one month, our company purchased expense software from this same accounting firm. What on earth had happened? As I started to investigate, I realized that the sales team had liked the team from this accounting software and had thought their software worked well in the demo. In the next week, over lunch, by the coffee machine, and by the water cooler, the sales team members would chat with their friends in accounting about the demo. It was if the sales team had caught a virus and was spreading it through the organization! I was blown away. At the end of the day, the company that had effectively marketed to our entire organization was the one that won the account. I decided to take a page from this accounting software company's book and see how it worked with my account-based marketing approach. It turns out that it worked like a charm.

Now, I'm not advocating that you canvass every single person at every single one of your ICP accounts. There's not enough time in the world to do that, and account-based marketing is all about operating as efficiently as possible. However, this is an incredibly powerful approach to take for accounts that are towards the bottom of your funnel. Once an account gets close to a decision-making process, this is a great tool to use.

This approach intends to be everywhere with a company. As they start to compare your solution to your competitors', you want to be at the top of the decision-maker's mind. But you are not the only one talking to the decision-maker. The decision-maker is talking to their friends throughout the company on a daily basis. Why not enlist these other members of the team as part of your campaign? Find a way to be the talk of the water cooler. You'll start to occupy more of the mindshare of your decision maker than any other organization. And when it comes time for to make a decision, you're more likely than not to be the one they select.

In the next chapter, we're going to expand on this point. This final element of this book is about being everywhere at once, and always being on the top of your target profile's mind.

Key takeaways:
- You are not just selling to your decision-maker; you are selling to an organization. People within an organization compare notes and influence each other. Don't limit yourself to just selling to the decision-maker. Find ways to get in front of multiple parts of an organization, and you'll increase your probability of success.
- This tactic is time-consuming and so it's best to reserve it for those accounts that are towards the bottom of your pipeline. Wait until they are in the decision-making phase to kick this step into high gear.

Step 12: Take the Oxygen Out of the Room

"Only those who will risk going too far can possibly find out how far one can go."
— **T.S. Eliot**

The best comment I've ever heard from a prospect-turned-client was this: "you guys are everywhere, and buying your software didn't seem like a choice."

I always thought of our addressable market as an out of control fire, the flames being the individual target accounts. It moves unpredictably. It constantly consumes different products, using each product as a fuel for the fire while never putting it out. The question then becomes: how do you manage the fire, block off the fire, and put it out? Putting out the fire is what I call account control. When you put out the fire, your potential customer becomes your partner, and they are roaming the countryside, looking for an alternative solution.

Taking the oxygen out of the room means just that – there are no more burning flames of desire to start another software search. This isn't some parlor trick to distract your potential customer and convince them to look the other way when new and exciting alternative solutions come up. Instead, it is all about becoming a trusted advisor who can help your potential customer navigate these inevitable developments. How do you do that? By making sure that your product and product marketing are aligned with the overall vision and destination of the client.

You have hit the pinnacle of marketing when you can carve out a product category for yourself. No longer are you competing with the masses; you are in a product category of one. Here, you get to define the rules. Here, there is no competitive matrix. That's the goal, the result, of account-based marketing. It is the point at which your customers know you, trust you and love you. Instead of delivering a stagnant (or dead) product, you deliver a vibrant, constantly-evolving product that solves more and more of their problems over time. This leads to the most enjoyable phase of account-based marketing: product line methodology.

What is the product line methodology?

The watershed moment in account-based marketing takes place when you achieve the product line methodology. This occurs only once you have become proficient at solving a subset of problems for your target accounts. Once you achieve this, you have permission to take the positive brand equity you've built and expand your empire. You do this by making new products that solve a different set of problems for each of the different personas at your target account. Remember, in all

Remember, in all likelihood, you are not the only software vendor your customers are using. They are spending money with other vendors because they have multiple problems that need to be solved. If you can offer these solutions, your customer is not only going to save money but you will also be reducing the bureaucratic nightmare of managing multiple contracts, vendors, systems, and points of contact.

You've seen this game play out many times on larger scales. One example is Oracle's progression from a database company expanding into an ERP company as well. Another example is Salesforce, moving from a CRM company and expanding into marketing automation as well. This is the next logical step of a rapidly growing and evolving organization. Companies that only have a single product get acquired by larger companies. On the other hand, multi-product companies go public and live on far past the lifecycle of the initial product they released.

While all the nuances of the product line methodology cannot be captured in the confines of this book, here are a few things to remember:

1. More than likely, your company's journey started with one product. This core product is the roots of your company, and just like family, you should never forget or abandon this core product. Always be honest with yourself; if you do not have money and resources to expand your product line, do not try to expand. Overextending will invariably damage your core market. However, never forget that having only a single

However, never forget that having only a single product at your company places an expiration date on your company.

2. The next logical product for your company isn't necessarily an expansion of product functionality from your base product. This is one of the biggest difficulties that companies face in finding their next product, and it is entirely self-imposed. Your next product may be completely unrelated to your core product. Instead of expecting it to be an extension of your first product, maintain one simple limitation: it must solve the problem for a different persona **at the same** target account. This overlap of different personas at the same account is the holy grail of upselling your customer and expanding your product line.

3. Eventually, you will have two to three products. Do not stumble at this point by trying to develop a strategy around bundling your products together. Product line methodology is not about creating products that you can place side-by-side in a "good, better, best" scenario. The automobile industry is a classic example of the product line methodology. An automobile company can release a world-class truck and sell this to a lady to use in her workplace. At the same time, the same automobile company can also release a world-class sedan and sell this to that lady's daughter. The automobile company is sold to two different customer personas within the same household. However, the two products they are

selling are drastically different— they are not a progression, but rather focus on solving entirely different needs.

4. Make sure that you have product and product marketing alignment. In my career, I have always run Product Marketing, and in some cases, Product. Product Marketing has never been the slickest department where I have worked.
    Product Marketing shouldn't be viewed simply as the brochure-generating department. Rather, Product Marketing should be all about evaluating market opportunities for Product and then helping assign resources to build the next great product. Alignment is non-negotiable for this to work.

It's Time for a Product Category

If you can find a way to move from being a product company to a platform company, you've reached the pinnacle. The only way to do that is by earning market share in multiple product lines while at the same time becoming a data hub for other products that may not have the brand equity or strategy to integrate. Once you become the platform of your target markets, you should be at the stage in which your company has a significant footprint. Launching a product category is a marketer's dream—it means getting to the point where you are now the market maker. In this capacity, you define the rules. But don't take this lightly—this is a hard mantle to keep up with and not an easy one to implement.

Words of Warning

Remember, once you have everyone's attention, it's up to you to know what to do with it. Also keep in mind that you are going to be scrutinized and likely attacked by competitors. If you are inauthentic or the company is not aligned, it's only a matter of time before the entire target audience knows, and you become known as an "also-ran."

Be everywhere. Everywhere that your ICP looks, you want them to see your company. Every place your ICP is reading, you want them to find information about your brand. Whatever your ICP is listening to, you want them to hear about your software. Be omnipresent in their life.

This is no longer just about closing the deal. It's about retaining business and reducing your churn. Even when the client is listed on Closed Won, you still want them to be thinking about you. The moment they stop thinking about you is the moment they're susceptible to being stolen away by a competitor.

This is yet another area for creativity. Purchase a billboard on the routes to and from your key accounts commute. Sponsor the golf tournaments they want to attend. Buy ads on the podcasts they listen to most. Take a page from our book and sew your ads into the magazines headed their way! Be like family to your ICP. Understand that you need to build a renewal journey. This renewal journey needs to be in place before you even close the deal. This journey never stops; you always need to be front and center in their attention.

At this point, we have covered the twelve steps to help you succeed with account-based marketing. Next, I would like to share a few lessons that I've learned in the last eighteen years to help you avoid some common pitfalls.

Key takeaways:
- Perfect the product line methodology. You need a second and third product to survive as a company, but these products do not need to be extensions of each other. Rather, they need to solve the problem of a different customer persona within the same account.
- Think about your renewal journey before you even close the account. Maintaining your key clients is as important, if not more important, than gaining the account in the first place.
- Be creative and find ways to be constantly in front of your ICP. Billboards, podcast advertisements, event sponsorship, and even print ads are all weapons at your disposal. You're only limited by your creativity and understanding of your ICP.

Lessons Learned & Mistakes to Avoid

"Mistakes are the growing pains of wisdom."
— William George Jordan

I have made more than my fair share of mistakes throughout my career. This is all part of learning. Experimentation is vital to your company's growth, and if you are experimenting—if you are pushing and expanding the borders of account-based marketing—mistakes are inevitable. It is crucial that you adopt a learning mindset so that you can adapt and respond to your failures. This is the only way forward. If you want to be even more efficient, you can learn from the mistakes of others. So here are five mistakes that I have made, as well as what I have learned from them.

Mistake #1: Not involving the customer success team when you create an ideal customer profile

By this point, you know that the ideal customer profile is the cornerstone of account-based marketing. If you have an exceptional ICP, you can expect exceptional results. However, this also follows the age-old adage of "garbage in, garbage out." If your ideal customer profile is not accurate, then every single step that follows will be flawed, inefficient, and ultimately doomed.

I have developed some incredibly intricate and accurate ICPs. But I have had more than my fair share of colossal failures as well. After my tenth or twentieth ICP blow-up, I took a step back to do a post-mortem. What on earth was going wrong in the ICPs that didn't take root? After an exhaustive analysis, I realized an astoundingly consistent trend. Every single ICP that I developed and then failed to perform had one thing in common: the customer success team had a minimal (or sometimes completely absent) presence as part of the process. Often, I was in a rush and need to get ready for our next agile planning process. I had a good sense of who our customers were and what they were like, so I'd skipped a step. It turns out that this skipped step was the secret ingredient. I was shocked at how consistently true this was.

My advice to you is to take your time as you're developing your ICP. Every time. I have completed hundreds of ICPs. But I know this lesson learned is accurate, and so I still take the time to involve my customer success team every time. They offer a wealth of knowledge and insights, and without their input, your ICP is doomed.

Mistake #2: Using anecdotal information rather than actual data

I may have spent less than a year in finance, but this early part of my career has stuck with me. It's all about the numbers. The more you work with account-based marketing, the more tempting it will be to "shoot from the hip" and use anecdotes. You have a sense of how one of your clients is doing, so you can wing it and ballpark the impact you've had, right? Wrong.

Just like a good detective, your never-ending mantra needs to be "Just the facts, ma'am." Stick to the data, the real results, and the measured impact. Trust me on this. Even if you can spin a tremendous yarn and tell an incredible story, nothing will have a bigger impact than actual data. Time and time again, I've seen that when my team or I stray from using actual data, our results start to decline. Don't make this mistake—stick to the data. It demonstrates that you are a professional and a leader in your industry. Don't take the short-cut to use sloppy anecdotes.

Mistake #3: Not interviewing clients directly across their organization

Are you noticing a trend here? Every single mistake so far is the result of rushing a step. Mistake #1 came about when I rushed through the Ideal Customer Profile step. Mistake #2 came about when I rushed through crunching the numbers. It's the same with Mistake #3, which comes about when you rush through getting to know your clients and prospective customers.

Every single organization is unique. There are decision-makers who hold positional power, and more important people who influence all the key stakeholders. You cannot rely on the title, and you cannot rely on gut feeling. During the selling process, you need to intimately get to know the organization to which you are selling. The moment you think that you've "seen this before," you're destined for heartbreak. Take the extra time to interview a variety of clients across the organization. This is the only way—and I mean the ONLY way—to truly understand the organization. I guarantee that you will be surprised every single time. The person you may overlook or think is insignificant will be the biggest component in closing the deal. Sometimes, the person who you believe you need to convince isn't really respected in the organization, and their endorsement may actually be the kiss of death for your deal. Don't rush—take your time and be thorough in your interviews. Like most things in account-based marketing, it will cost you more time upfront but will save you a significant amount of time later in the process.

Mistake #4: Getting stuck in an echo chamber and losing perspective

If you follow the twelve steps in this book, your organization is going to grow. Quickly. But there is nothing more dangerous than a little success. It causes most to become over-confident and to forget the truths that got them to that point. As you grow your team, many of your new hires will hold you in high esteem. They are likely to go along with what you suggest or trust you implicitly. And that can feel good. I imagine that the frog in the slowly boiling pot of water may feel like he's in a luxurious Jacuzzi before he meets his untimely end.

Be aware of your success. Find ways to keep your team honest about what is working and honest about what is not working. No matter how smart or successful you become, you will always need a fresh set of eyes. Reward your team for playing devil's advocate—this is never an enjoyable role to play. I have even seen organizations in which one person is randomly assigned to be the devil's advocate during each meeting. This person has to push back; they have to ask the hard questions; they need to be the skeptic. This is great because it helps institutionalize the need for a fresh set of eyes. The alternative is to live in an echo chamber in which everyone reinforces your ideas. This is a hallmark of a company headed for destruction. Avoid it by maintaining fresh eyes for every project.

Mistake #5: Choosing quick revenue versus long-term growth

I know this is the toughest of all mistakes because I have been lulled towards this destructive siren more times than I can count. Things move quickly in a startup. I joke with my friends that one year at a startup is the same as ten years in an established company. You learn more, you move faster, and it can feel like you're driving a Ferrari. There are so many tempting shortcuts on the way to success. In fact, to succeed you need to exploit every conceivable shortcut you can find. In many ways, account-based marketing is all about finding and exploiting shortcuts—it's about hacking your way to faster and more efficient growth. I wouldn't be where I am now without hacking these shortcuts week in and week out.

That's not what I'm talking about here. I'm talking about making those decisions that meet our revenue goal this month by closing a deal with a customer we know isn't the right fit for our software. There are always extenuating circumstances: we have to look good for tomorrow's board meeting; we're raising money and need to show continuous growth; we need to boost this sales person's self-esteem so he can sell even more. It is always infuriatingly difficult to say no to this quick revenue. In my experience, it has always been a mistake to say yes. The revenue we gain costs us ten times more regarding time, money, and pain. I have made decisions like this at least a dozen times in my career. Without exception, I regret every single one of them.

Do yourself, your team, and your company a favor. Decide to do what is best for the organization in the long-term. Period. You will always need goals and short-term measures of progress. Break through walls to achieve these, but never sacrifice long-term growth to gain short-term revenue.

The Tech Stack

"The advance of technology is based on making it fit in so that you don't really even notice it, so it's part of everyday life."
-- Bill Gates

Not a day goes by when there isn't a new solution or marketing technology product that offers marketers a simple and easy way to make more money with the same amount of investment in marketing. The reality is that there is no easy way out, and technology is only as good as the process it's being implemented against. That's right: I'm not aiming to suggest the next great solution you need to buy or the technology that you need to have installed because there isn't just one answer.

What matters is the process you use in marketing and how you implement your account-based marketing. It is up to you to tightly align your team's objectives, goals, and process outcomes. All that technology can do is take
your alignment and accelerate what you would otherwise accomplish. Technology cannot do the heavy lifting of creating the right goals and coordinating the right people. But it can help speed up this
process… some of the time. Other times, technology can slow down and even prevent progress.

Countless times, I've seen this problem when I've advised companies. The problem is a very common oversight. When I speak with these teams, they have a clear understanding of the investment they will need to make in the technology and the technology implementation. They have vetted multiple vendors around these criteria and are about to go ahead (or worse yet, have already moved forward with a solution). What each of these teams has in common is that they overlook a vital cost component: software upkeep. To effectively leverage software, you need a marketing ops organization behind them who can help their team optimize the use of their software.

That being said, there is technology that can help you as you implement an account-based marketing approach. I would like to highlight a few of the most important types of technology that can help in this regard.

Customer Relationship Management (CRM) Software

The first place you need to start is with a good CRM system. Most people that I know are running Salesforce, but that's not the only one out there. There are very, very good CRM systems that might not even cost you much. It's not so much about the system, but more about how you track data in your CRM. Your CRM should be used for data hygiene. Think about it: You could have the best CRM system that money can buy, but if the data stored within it is incorrect, it does you no good. Worse (and more common), if your CRM relies on a human to update it, you're going to end up with a significant amount of missing information that will make it impossible to run a successful marketing and sales organization.

Your CRM is a vessel for account opportunity, contact data, and notes. How you use your CRM is more important than what your CRM is. My recommendation is first to always lockdown the thermographic data on each account. Second, make it more updatable by a human. Third, have a hygiene tool run through your CRM system on a regular basis, validating things like industry, revenue, and some employees. Many providers have data about each of these fields. Many of these data providers do not charge much for this information. My intention in this section of the book is not to provide you with a list of names; the names will change from one year to the next. More importantly, I intend to remind you that regardless of what CRM system you choose, your CRM is only as good as the data you put into it. Garbage in, garbage out.

Account Discovery Software

There has been this new term thrown around quite a bit called Account Discovery, or more specifically Artificial Intelligence Account Discovery. Artificial intelligence (AI) is a big term that appears often in marketing. What AI aims to do is help you identify companies for outreach. They do this (or claim to do it) by analyzing the closed dormant accounts in your CRM, and then find companies with similar characteristics. I only partially believe in this technology.

The reason I'm skeptical about this technology is that there are a lot of human elements and gut factors involved in this sort of analysis. We have provided extensive detail about this in the sections on ICP planning, and by now you now that ICP discovery is an important aspect of your marketing organization. Furthermore, it replaces that awful term "lead velocity," because new accounts feed the machine, grow your market, and ultimately grow revenue. There are great solutions out there that will look at your Closed Won list, analyze the data, and spit out accounts or companies that are of equal or better match. Again, it's worth noting that this is only possible so long as the data in your CRM is accurate. However, this sort of technology is exceptional, and you will want to implement something similar to it.

Account discovery is the job of technology, of scrapers, of smart LinkedIn usage, but it's also the job of this emerging artificial intelligence. Use the machines as much as possible to analyze your data, but always know that there is a human element that is just as important. You should validate the accounts that are coming up as exact matches and overlay them with the ICP model that you've created in the earlier chapters. In this way, you can blend technology with human intuition, a winning combination.

Marketing Attribution Software

Marketing attribution is in technology that most marketers use to beat their chest and say, "Look how good we're doing!" While this may feel good, it is a suboptimal use of this technology. Instead, Marketing attribution technology is best utilized to invest your dollars in the wisest way possible. If you don't know how your dollars result in sales or revenue, then how do you know how to allocate your money?

There are several different models out there in the world. One of my favorites is called Full Cycle. Full Cycle looks at a variety of important factors. What was the account's first touch? When was the account's first lead created? Was the account's first lead created with a target account or target contact? What was the last engagement before an opportunity being created? What was the last engagement before a Closed Won moment occurring? While nothing is perfect, at least knowing all of these aspects means that you will know every engagement you have with target accounts.

Remember, I started off doing this all in Excel, so I know that you can do that initially as well. You can graduate from Excel when you feel that you have fine-tuned your model and you are ready for the next level. It is as simple as this: you need a system to track attribution. Consider the amount of money that you would save if you knew what was working and what wasn't working. The danger of marketing attribution is that you might put too much faith in the fact that certain things don't work. You need to be able to validate which touches most impacted the opportunity.

The best way to do that is to always to talk to a client. However, as you have these client conversations, you need a system to track all the marketing activities and assign them to the relevant accounts, people, opportunities, and ultimately to the revenue generated. This is a lot of work. I know great companies that have done custom attribution solutions. Ultimately, it's a matter of tying together all of your tools, putting them in one place. It's a matter of tracking all of your marketing activities and then linking these activities to how successful they've been.

Marketing Automation Software

I believe that "marketing automation" is a misnomer. The idea that there is one solution for everything has not played out appropriately. The reality is that marketing automation is just really emailed automation. If you remember earlier, I mentioned that email automation has to be intelligent, and it must be based on behavioral activity. As a result, I have listed marketing automation as fourth on my list of technologies.

Behavioral activity is rooted in attribution, so marketing attribution data is a precursor to creating a smart lead nurture system. A smart lead nurture system drives an inordinate amount of email activity and should result in a very, very successful email channel in which people are clicking through, interacting and purchasing. Ultimately, you want to make sure your highest-value people are assigned to your highest-value accounts. You can use the marketing automation software to refine the automated process through which these emails are sent, and through which the accounts are assigned to the correct individuals in your team.

As I've said, marketing automation is email-sending. There are some great tools that are very expensive, but there are also some great tools that aren't. Additionally, there are a variety of new technologies that are coming up through the market. As you evaluate these new technologies, the first thing I would ask any email platform is, "Show me your workflow engine and show me how smart you can make your workflows based on behavioral data. How many paths can you start?" If those things are difficult, or if you can't track performance at the account level, walk away from the technology. Marketing automation is a misnomer, just like Enterprise Resource Planning (ERP) was. Having one solution for all things is not practical. Choose the right email tool, don't overspend, don't allocate too much of your marketing technology budget with it, and track success all the way through. Again, it's not the tool; it's how you run the tool that matters. Make sure that you don't overspend on an email marketing platform.

Social Software

Social management is hard. There are a lot of channels, which makes attribution difficult. There's both organic and paid social, each of which results in different metrics. Engagement can be hard to track. Sentiment analysis and what is being said about you in the market is important. All of these things make your social platform almost as important as your email platform.

In my opinion, the B2B industry does not successfully leverage social. We've gone and posted tweets, we've published LinkedIn articles, and we've even dabbled with Facebook. In each of these platforms, we try to create some call to action in order to create demand. It doesn't work because most articles are shallow and driven around by the premise of "Hey, buy my software." The reality is that you need to go back to that contact stage and say, "If I'm building awareness in my company, but I want to do it in a way as a good citizen of the industry, what information should I be giving people through social, rather than taking away?"

The "me first/buy my software" social plan is consistently the largest error I see brands making. The sole purpose of their social content is to convince someone to buy their software. It would be far more effective to use social media to provide value to your community. Give them a learning moment, and they'll appreciate it, understand your brand and come back. Social media is about building a relationship, not always going for the kill. This is where social management systems are the most helpful because they allow your team to track your social content. They will allow you to track your engagement metrics and see which content is driving the most shares and engagements. In this way, social management systems are as important as content management solutions. Having the ability to pull out data quickly, pull out articles that make sense, and go with what works is not within the capabilities of Google Docs and spreadsheets.

I put together social and content management for a reason. Social media has a limited lifespan as does email, but content can live for a very long time. Content management systems are required to drive a huge impact on how much content you're producing. It's an important thing to note that there should be a word count target at your organization for the amount of content that you need to create every month. All those words need to go somewhere. Make sure that you have a content management system that drives not just the marketing department but also the content for the sales team to use through the sales cycle. Ultimately, your content customer success team should be able to use this content as well.

Numbers Don't Lie

*"Growth is never by mere chance; it is
the result of forces working together."*
— **James Cash Penney, founder of JC Penney**

I would like to conclude by sharing a few numbers (once
again, a nod to my roots in finance). When it comes to
Closed Won conversions, an account-based marketing
sourced lead is **four times more likely** to convert than a
lead sourced by any other means. In my companies,
over 84% of all Closed Won opportunities were sourced
through account-based marketing. Through this method,
I have achieved a **600%** marketing return on investment.
Enough said.

About the Author

Bassem Hamdy is the Founder & CEO of wokeABM, a boutique consulting firm that specializes in ABM marketing in B2B SaaS companies. Bassem has over 18 years of experience in the construction software industry and actively attends industry events as a thought leader and speaker. A trusted resource for business process improvement, Bassem is an innovative leader, constantly pushing boundaries and producing creative solutions. Bassem received his BComm. from McMaster University in Canada.

"Bassem is a strategic thinker and supported the executive staff in developing our growth strategy. He has an exceptional presentation, story-telling, and writing skills. When asked, most people describe him as "brilliant" because his creativity is boundless."
-- Tooey C., CEO of Procore

"Having worked with Bassem in the past, I can say confidently that Bassem has a special skill set. There are people that can share a vision, there are people that can create plans, and there are people that can action those plans. It is rare to find someone that can do all."
-- Casey S., VP of Aconex

Made in the USA
Columbia, SC
22 March 2021